*A Theory of*
*Psychological Reactance*

# SOCIAL PSYCHOLOGY

A series of monographs, treatises, and texts

Edited by

Leon Festinger
Department of Psychology
Stanford University
Stanford, California

and

Stanley Schachter
Department of Social Psychology
Columbia University
New York, New York

*Jack W. Brehm,* **A Theory of Psychological Reactance. 1966**

# A Theory of
# Psychological Reactance

JACK W. BREHM

DEPARTMENT OF PSYCHOLOGY
DUKE UNIVERSITY
DURHAM, NORTH CAROLINA

ACADEMIC PRESS · New York · London 1966

ACADEMIC PRESS INC.
111 Fifth Avenue, New York, New York 10003

*United Kingdom Edition published by*
ACADEMIC PRESS INC. (LONDON) LTD.
Berkeley Square House, London W.1

LIBRARY OF CONGRESS CATALOG CARD NUMBER: 66-27018

PRINTED IN THE UNITED STATES OF AMERICA

# Preface

Why is it that a child sometimes does the opposite of what he is told? Why would a person sometimes dislike receiving a favor? Why is propaganda frequently ineffective in persuading people? And why would the grass in the adjacent pasture ever appear greener? There may be no single explanation for any one of these questions and surely there is no single explanation for all of them together. Nevertheless, it is possible to construct an explanation which, in effect, ties together these rather heterogeneous phenomena. The purpose of this monograph is to propose one such explanation along with relevant experimental evidence.

Because the explanation to be outlined concerns the notion of freedom, and many disciplines have a vested interest in this notion, it may be well to indicate at the beginning some of the things which this monograph is not. It is not a philosophical treatise, a political, legal, or economic essay, nor a sociological analysis of social movements. It is not even intended as a psychological analysis of "freedom demonstrations," although there is a coincidental relationship. With these traditional treatments of freedom ruled out, what can this monograph be concerned with? The answer is simple: the multifarious freedoms of daily living and how the individual responds when these freedoms are threatened or eliminated.

If there is anything surprising about a theory concerning how people respond to elimination of freedom it is that such a theory has not been proposed earlier. For given the historical concern of our culture for freedoms of one kind or another, and given the current plethora of freedom demonstrations, it seems obvious that concern for freedom should have some general psychological implications. But perhaps the concern for freedom has been so dramatic that it has obscured the possibility of less obvious and more general implications. After all, it is quite apparent that humans are frequently upset when they feel deprived of major political and economic freedoms — and this is neither surprising nor in apparent need of explanation. What may not be so obvious is that less salient restrictions of freedom are a pervasive aspect of daily life.

The present work grew not out of observation of the individual's concern for political or economic freedoms but rather out of an attempt to understand certain phenomena of interpersonal relations. For example, my wife, Lee, and I jointly noticed that there were occasional instances in which advice given by one person to another had negative rather than positive influence. This seemed to be true no matter how benign the apparent motives of the person giving the advice, and no matter which side of a decision the advice supported. This kind of negative influence is fairly common and is normally explained in terms of personality factors and/or social power. Neither type of analysis seemed satisfactory, however, since our informal observations indicated that the negative influence tendency occurred with different kinds of people and in different kinds of power relationships. After several weeks of casual cogitation it struck me that the solution to the problem might be very simple indeed; what the individual wanted was the freedom to make up his own mind, and any advice would interfere with this freedom no matter which side the advice supported and, within a broad range, no matter who gave the advice. The negative influence, then, was conceived as an attempt on the part of the individual to re-establish his freedom to decide for himself.

During the approximately three ensuing years the theory has been delineated, broadened, and elaborated, and with the help of several undergraduate and graduate students, it has been subjected to a variety of empirical tests. Needless to say, the development of the theory and the program of testing were not as neat and systematic as would appear from this monograph. For example, our early concern was primarily with social influence and it was only considerably later that we explored the more basic effects of nonsocial restrictions of freedom. Also, we do not report our complete failures in which we found that we did not understand sufficiently well how to create freedom in a laboratory setting, nor how to measure responses to threats or eliminations of freedom. While the theoretical statement is still somewhat fuzzy in places and has not yet been thoroughly tested, it has received empirical support from the majority of the tests we have made. It is my hope that the theory is now sufficiently clear so that others may test implications which they find interesting or useful.

*Durham, North Carolina*                    JACK W. BREHM

*July, 1966*

# Acknowledgments

The development of the theory has benefited from the interest and critical comments of a number of people over the last few years. First and foremost, I would like to thank my wife, Lee, who in addition to helping to isolate the fundamental phenomenon, has given encouragement, suggestions and critical comment throughout my pursuit of the problem. Second, in the early stages of the work when the ideas were vague and considerable courage was necessary to attempt an experiment, Ann Himelick Cole and Judith Weiner Regan provided the enthusiasm and intellectual prowess to get things going. Their part was invaluable. A number of other people have been helpful by their interest and critical comments at one time or another. In particular, I should like to thank Nickolas Cottrell, Claude Faucheux, the late Robert Formica, Jonathan Freedman, Herbert Greenwald, Thomas Hammock, Barbara Burton Hewett, Joseph Mancusi, Dorothy McQuown, Paul Seder, John Sensenig, Janet Shaban, Lloyd Stires, and Robert Wicklund.

For comments and suggestions on one or more parts of the manuscript for this monograph I would like to thank several of the above named people and also Chester Insko, Darwyn Linder, Judson Mills, Harold Schiffman, John Schopler, Kelly Shaver, Elaine Walster, and Robert Zajonc.

Finally, Leon Festinger, Edward E. Jones, and Peter Schönbach have all been very generous and helpful not only for providing detailed comments upon the entire manuscript but also for discussion of various points relevant to the development of the theory. Their contributions are deeply appreciated.

Much of the experimental work was made possible by the generous cooperation of the Public School Systems of Durham and Durham County. For their help in this work I would like to thank Mr. Lew

Hannen, Superintendent of Durham Schools; Mr. E. L. Phillips, Assistant Superintendent of Durham Schools; Mrs. Ruth L. McRacken, Director of Elementary Education for Durham Schools; and Mr. Charles H. Chewning, Superintendent of Durham County Schools.

I wish gratefully to acknowledge that support for the initial phase of this research was provided by the National Science Foundation, and current support is provided by the National Institute of Mental Health as well as by small grants from the General Electric Company and the Duke University Research Council.

I wish to thank the Academic Press for permission to reproduce material from the *Journal of Experimental Social Psychology,* the American Psychological Association for permission to reproduce material from the *Journal of Applied Psychology* and the *Journal of Personality and Social Psychology,* and the Duke University Press for permission to reproduce material from the *Journal of Personality.*

To my secretary, Mrs. Carole Shaver, I give sincere thanks for her efficient and accurate handling of the manuscript.

# Contents

# CHAPTER I

# A Theory of Psychological Reactance

Freedom of behavior is a pervasive and important aspect of human life. People are continually surveying their internal and external states of affairs and making decisions about what they will do, how they will do it, and when they will do it. They consider their wants and needs, the dangers and benefits available in their surroundings, and the ways in which they can accomplish various ends. This is not to say that behavior is always freely selected. It will frequently be true that individuals perform given acts without quite knowing why, and it will also be true that they perform acts because they knew they were not free to do otherwise. Nevertheless, most of the time people will feel that they are relatively free to engage in a variety of different behaviors and that they can select among these as they please.

There is good reason for the belief that one has freedom of action. Objectively there frequently are multiple possibilities, and subjectively there are frequently multiple needs, none of which demands immediate gratification. Thus, subjectively at least, it seems that one scans the possibilities and their effects, and then decides which of the several possibilities to take. Whether or not a person "really" has freedom, he can and almost certainly will believe that he has.

The freedom to choose when and how to behave is potentially beneficial. To the extent a person is aware of his needs and the behaviors necessary to satisfy those needs, and providing he has the appropriate freedom, he can choose behaviors so as to maximize need satisfaction. An individual, for example, who felt more thirsty than hungry and who, at the moment, was free to go either to a soda fountain or a restaurant, could satisfy his dominant need by choosing to go to the soda fountain.

Without the freedom to select behaviors appropriate to various needs, the satisfaction of needs would be a more haphazard affair which would not only fail to maximize need satisfaction but could frequently result in extreme deprivation, pain, and even death. Given some minimal level of valid knowledge about oneself and the environment, freedom to choose among different behavioral possibilities will generally help one to survive and thrive.

It is reasonable to assume, then, that if a person's behavioral freedom is reduced or threatened with reduction, he will become motivationally aroused. This arousal would presumably be directed against any further loss of freedom and it would also be directed toward the re-establishment of whatever freedom had already been lost or threatened. Since this hypothetical motivational state is in response to the reduction (or threatened reduction) of one's potential for acting, and conceptually may be considered a counterforce, it will be called "psychological reactance." The purpose of this volume, then, is to delineate a theory of psychological reactance and to report and examine relevant evidence.

Before presenting a formal theoretical statement, it may be well to consider two hypothetical examples of the arousal and reduction of reactance. Picture first Mr. John Smith, who normally plays golf on Sunday afternoons, although occasionally he spends Sunday afternoon watching television or puttering around his workshop. The important point is that Smith always spends Sunday afternoon doing whichever of these three things he prefers; he is free to choose which he will do. Now consider a specific Sunday morning on which Smith's wife announces that Smith will have to play golf that afternoon since she has invited several of her ladyfriends to the house for a party. Mr. Smith's freedom is threatened with reduction in several ways: (1) he cannot watch television, (2) he cannot putter in his workshop, and (3) he must (Mrs. Smith says) play golf. According to the present view, Smith would be motivationally aroused to re-establish these threatened freedoms. We might therefore expect to hear him protest that there was an important television program he wanted to watch and that he had planned to do some special work in his shop. We might also expect to hear him say that he is tired of golf, that the course is not in good condition, and so forth. If the amount of reactance aroused were great, we might indeed expect Smith to spend the afternoon watching television, perhaps with the volume turned unusually high.

For a second hypothetical example, let us consider a person who is looking for a pack of cigarettes, and let us suppose that this person normally smokes Camels but also occasionally smokes Kools. Let us further suppose that on this occasion he would prefer to have Camels, and that he locates a vending machine which contains both Camels and Kools. After depositing the necessary amount of money in the machine, he is just about to reach out to pull the lever for Camels when the machine dispenses a pack of Camels. Since the machine could not have divined his preference, the individual's freedom to select his own brand has been pre-empted and he should experience reactance. We might expect this person to find suddenly that he is not so eager to have Camels, that if he now had his choice he might well select Kools or some other kind, and that he is displeased with vending machines. He might even put more money in the machine in order to select a pack of Kools.

It is important to note that neither of these hypothetical examples involves simple frustration, i.e., blocking of the person from his preferred goal. Mr. Smith was likely to play golf anyway, and we may even make it a condition of the example that he intended to play golf prior to his wife's announcing that he had to. Similarly, the man seeking Camels received just what he was looking for. But in both cases, according to the present proposal, these people should be motivationally aroused to resist doing or taking what they originally intended. We shall return to this point again. For the present, since a better picture has been gained through these examples of somewhat trivial events of what is meant by reactance, let us turn to a formal statement of the determinants and consequences of psychological reactance.

## The Theory

It is assumed that for a given person at a given time, there is a set of behaviors any one of which he could engage in either at the moment or at some time in the future. This set may be called the individual's "free behaviors." Free behaviors include only acts that are realistically possible: smoking a cigarette could be a free behavior, while walking to the moon could not. Behaviors may become free in a variety of ways. A person may become free to spend company money for lunches by formal agreement between himself and the company; a person may acquire the freedom to read a book by learning how to read; one may feel free to spit on the walk because one always has done so; and one may feel free to vote because the right is guaranteed by law. In general, we may say that for specified behaviors to be free, the individual must have the relevant physical and psychological abilities to engage in them, and he must know, by experience, by general custom, or by formal agreement, that he may engage in them.

It should be noted that the concept of "behavior" is intended to include any conceivable act. A behavior might consist of selecting a choice alternative, thinking that Roosevelt was a good president, or not watching television. More generally, behaviors may be characterized as "what one does (or doesn't)," "how one does something," or "when one does something."

It will not always be clear either to an objective observer or to the individual himself whether or not he has the freedom to engage in a given behavior. This can happen because the individual has inadequate relevant information, as when he lacks experience in attempting to engage in the behavior in question and neither does he know any formal relevant rules. Lack of clarity about freedom can also occur because there is conflicting information. A jaywalker, for example, may feel free to jaywalk because he frequently does so but he may not feel free to jaywalk because to do so is illegal. While these unclarities about when a behavior is or is not free may constitute serious difficulty for the analysis of practical problems, they do not preclude clear and adequate experimental tests of the theory, for it is possible to construct situations in which specified behavioral freedoms are relatively unequivocal.

*Given that a person has a set of free behaviors, he will experience reactance whenever any of those behaviors is eliminated or threatened with elimination.* That is, if a person felt free to engage in behaviors A, B, and C, and then learned that he could not engage in, for example, A, he would experience reactance.

The magnitude of reactance is a direct function of (1) the importance of the free behaviors which are eliminated or threatened, (2) the proportion of free behaviors eliminated or threatened, and (3) where there is only a threat of elimination of free behaviors, the magnitude of that threat. Let us consider each of these determinants in somewhat greater detail.

1. Given that a certain free behavior has been threatened or eliminated, *the more important is that free behavior to the individual, the greater will be the magnitude of reactance.* The importance of a given behavior is a direct function of the unique instrumental value which

that behavior has for the satisfaction of needs, multiplied by the actual or potential maximum magnitude of those needs. By unique is meant that no other behavior in the individual's repertoire of behaviors would satisfy the same need or set of needs. In other words, the importance of a free behavior derives from its necessity for the reduction of potentially important needs. However, it is *not* necessary for the relevant needs to be of great magnitude at all times for the free behavior to have high importance at all times. It is only necessary that the individual believe he *might* have the needs in question. This may become more clear if we recall the example of Mr. Smith, who was told by his wife to go play golf, and who according to the present view should therefore experience increased motivation to watch television or putter in his workshop. It was noted then, and may be reiterated here, that Smith may actually have preferred to play golf prior to his wife's pronouncement and, further, he may not, on that particular Sunday, have had an active interest in watching television or puttering. But to the extent that he believes he *might* have wanted to do either of these things, the freedom to engage in them is important and the loss of that freedom should arouse reactance.

1a. The magnitude of reactance is also a direct function of the relative importance of the eliminated or threatened behavioral freedom compared to the importances of other freedoms of the moment. Considering all of a person's free behaviors at a given time, and holding constant the absolute importance of the one which is eliminated or threatened, its relative importance increases as the absolute importance of the other freedoms decreases.

In illustration, let us suppose that a person has rated several items on an equal interval scale where 0 equals no attraction and 100 equals very high attraction, and that the items A, B, etc., have received the following ratings: $A = 10$, $B = 20$, $C = 30$, $X = 70$, $Y = 80$, and $Z = 90$. Here the absolute attractiveness of X, Y, and Z is greater than that of A, B, and C, and if a person had the choice alternatives X, Y, and Z, and then lost Z, he would experience more reactance than if he had the alternatives A, B, and C, and then lost C. But if the absolute attractiveness of the eliminated alternative is held constant, then its relative attractiveness will determine the magnitude of reactance. If the individual had the choice alternatives A, B, and C and then lost B, he would experience more reactance than if he had the alternatives, A, B, and X, and then lost B. When one's choice alternatives are an orange, an apple, and a pear, he should experience a noticeable degree of reactance when someone swipes the apple; but when the choice alternatives are an orange, an apple and an automobile, one will not care much about the loss of the apple.

2. Given the individual's set of free behaviors, *the greater is the proportion eliminated or threatened with elimination, the greater will be the magnitude of reactance.* If a person believed himself free to engage in behaviors A, B, C, and D, all of which have some importance, then the elimination of both A and B would create more reactance than would the elimination of either A or B alone. Or, given that behavior A is eliminated, if the original set of free behaviors consisted of A and B there will be more reactance than if the original set consisted of A, B, C, and D.

3. Given that an important free behavior has been threatened with elimination, *the greater is the threat, the greater will be the magnitude of reactance.* A threat becomes greater as the likelihood increases that it could and would be carried out. A threat of the elimination of a free behavior will frequently be located in a social source, i.e., another person. When the threat is social, the question of how great the threat is will center on the formal and informal relationships between the threatener and the person threatened. Those who have equal or greater amounts of social power than oneself can issue threats of relatively great magnitude to one's own free behaviors, while those with less power would be relatively unable to muster serious threats.

3a. When a person's free behavior, A, is eliminated or threatened with elimination, there may also be the implication to him that other free behaviors, say B and C, or the same behavior on future occasions, $A_2$ and $A_3$, will also be eliminated. That is, by the loss of a single free behavior there may be by implication a threat of elimination of other free behaviors either in the present or in the future. This proposition assumes, of course, that the free behaviors in question are ordered such that the loss of one implies the loss of others. The ordering may be as simple as membership in a class. For example, if a secretary were informed she was not to chew gum while at work, she might easily imagine that other similar behaviors, such as smoking and sucking on candies would also be eliminated. Or, the dimension of implication might be such that elimination of a given behavior would imply the loss of some but not all related behaviors. Imagine, for example, a set of perquisites which correlates with job status at a hypothetical college.

Assistant professors have unlimited library privileges, associate professors have the same plus an office all to themselves, and full professors have these two advantages plus a graduate assistant to help them in their work. Under these conditions if a full professor were informed that he would no longer have an office to himself, he should also feel that his having a graduate assistant was in jeopardy though he would presumably feel there was relatively little threat of his losing library privileges.

3b. Just as a free behavior may be threatened by virtue of elimination of or threat to another free behavior, so a free behavior may be threatened by the elimination of or threat to another person's free behavior. The implication in this case relates the observed person to oneself; if the loss of a free behavior to an observed person could just as well happen to oneself, then one's own free behavior is threatened. When an observed person loses a free behavior similar to a free behavior for oneself, the greater is the implication that the loss could as easily have happened to oneself, the greater will be the magnitude of the reactance. If, for example, co-equal secretaries worked together in an office and normally felt free to go to the water cooler for a drink whenever they felt like it, the elimination of this freedom for one should threaten the same freedom for others, leading to their experiencing reactance.

### Justification and Legitimacy

If Mr. Smith says to Mr. Brown "You cannot have Betty for baby-sitting this evening," when Mr. Brown might have wanted Betty, then Brown should experience reactance. It will be obvious, however, that Brown's reaction will be affected by the justification and/or legitimacy of Smith's interference. If Smith adds that Betty's mother has gone to the hospital for an emergency operation, thus justifying the restriction, Brown will not show a strong negative reaction. If Betty is a young teenager and Smith happens to be her father, then Smith can legitimately control Betty's activities and again, Brown is not likely to show a strong negative reaction.

Justification and legitimacy, however, are complicated variables from the point of view of reactance theory. They tend, on the one hand, to affect the magnitude or reactance aroused by the loss of a freedom, and they tend on the other hand, to affect restraints against the effects of reactance. Let us consider these in turn.

When person A tells person B what to do, and thereby threatens a specific freedom of the latter, there may or may not be further freedoms threatened by implication, as we have already seen. One possible effect of justification is to limit the threat to a specific behavior or set of behaviors. So if Smith says that he is interfering with Brown's expectations because of a personal emergency, this keeps Brown from imagining that Smith will likely interfere on future occasions as well. Fewer of Brown's behavioral freedoms have been threatened. In a similar way, legitimacy may indicate the set of behaviors threatened since there will be a general presumption that illegitimate interference with one's freedoms is less likely to occur. There is an additional implication in the notion of legitimacy of behavioral restriction that one's freedom was equivocal anyway. In the above example, if Betty is a young teenager, then Brown could never have been sure of his freedom to have her babysit since she is normally subject to restrictions from her parents. Conversely, an illegitimate attempt to restrict one's freedom may be capable of arousing a great deal of reactance since it may imply a threat to a large number of free behaviors. If Smith is *not* the father of Betty and has no more legitimate control over her than does Brown, then Smith's attempted interference (without justification) also carries the implication that Smith may well attempt similar interferences on future occasions. From Brown's point of view, if Smith gets away with this, what can't he get away with?

Although justification and legitimacy may be seen as affecting the magnitude of reactance aroused by a given elimination or threat, lack of justification and legitimacy are not necessary conditions for the occurrence of reactance. A loss of freedom no matter how well justified, should still create reactance. And if we bear in mind that legitimacy (formal rules, agreement, etc.) is only one of several sources of freedom, we can also say that a loss of freedom, no matter how legitimate, can also result in reactance.

How a person responds to reactance will doubtless be affected by both justification and legitimacy. In general, these conditions will create restraints against direct attempts at restoration of freedom. For this reason, these conditions will tend to give rise to attempts at indirect restoration of freedom, such as through behavioral or social implication, when that kind of restoration is possible.

In the above discussion we have attempted to show that although justification and legitimacy are powerful determinants of the magnitude of reactance, their total effects are complicated. They are therefore not particularly useful tools for the demonstration of reactance effects in research and they have not been employed in the research reported in this volume. Rather, our attempts have been to test reactance hypotheses with justification and legitimacy held constant.

## THE EFFECTS OF REACTANCE

Psychological reactance is conceived as a motivational state directed toward the re-establishment of the free behaviors which have been eliminated or threatened with elimination. Generally, then, a person who experiences reactance will be motivated to attempt to regain the lost or threatened freedoms by whatever methods are available and appropriate. It should be helpful, of course, to be somewhat more specific about the effects of reactance, and in the following paragraphs we shall indicate several distinguishable possibilities.

### The Phenomenology of Reactance

While there is no assumption that a person will necessarily be aware of reactance, it should be true that when he is, he will feel an increased amount of self-direction in regard to his own behavior. That is, he will feel that he can do what he wants, that he does not have to do what he doesn't want, and that at least in regard to the freedom in question, he is the sole director of his own behavior. If the magnitude of reactance is relatively great, the individual may be aware of hostile and aggressive feelings as well. In this connection it may be noted that reactance can be an "uncivilized" motivational state since it frequently is directed against the social acts of others. For this reason it would not be surprising to find that a person in whom reactance has been aroused would tend to deny that he was either motivated to restore freedom or upset, and he might even convince himself of this. This tendency to defend against reactance can be expected to extend to nonverbal behavior as well. As will be seen, the studies in support of reactance theory have tended to use measures which do not require people to be uncivilized, or they have measured relatively subtle uncivilized responses.

When reactance does not lead to "uncivilized" or antisocial behavior, it should tend to result in some awareness of one's increased motivation to have what was lost or threatened. That is, a person's desire for a given behavior, A, should increase as a consequence of its being eliminated, or threatened with elimination, from his set of free behaviors. Correspondingly, behavior A should appear to increase in attractiveness.

### Direct Re-establishment of Freedom

The greater is the magnitude of reactance, the more will the individual attempt to re-establish the freedom which has been lost or threatened. However, attempts at re-establishment can be expected to occur only to the extent that there is a realistic possibility of succeeding. In general, reactance will result in attempts at restoration of freedom when there is some equivocality about the elimination of the free behavior in question, or, in other words, where there has only been a threat of elimination. When the loss of a free behavior is irreversible, as when one's left arm has been amputated or one has been told to do something by a person with immense power over oneself, there will not normally be attempts at direct restoration.

Direct re-establishment of freedom means engaging in that behavior which one has learned one cannot or should not engage in. If behavior A has been free and one is then told not to engage in A, the resultant reactance will lead the individual to engage in A. If one's set of free behaviors consisted of A and B and one were then told to do A, the direct restoration of freedom would consist in doing B.

Where freedom is threatened by social pressure, reactance will lead one to resist that pressure. If an habitual smoker, for example, were told by a friend that he should stop smoking, the resultant reactance would operate against the otherwise persuasive effects of the friend's advice. Continuing to smoke at the same rate or at a greater rate would re-establish the freedom to smoke. Quite obviously, however, the direct social influence might be greater than the magnitude of reactance, in which case a compromise response of reduced smoking would occur.

### Re-establishment of Freedom by Implication

When there are restraints against the direct re-establishment of freedom, attempts at re-establishment by implication will occur where possible. Consider again, for example, the secretary who has learned she can no longer chew gum on the job. She can re-establish her freedom by engaging in other behaviors of the same class, e.g., sucking on candy or smoking, or better yet, she can engage in what she would assume to be even less acceptable behaviors such as putting on lipstick, combing her hair, or eating candy bars.

Freedom can also be re-established by social implication. If a person has lost a free behavior through social threat, then the engagement in a similar free behavior by another person like himself and "in the same boat" will tend to re-establish his own freedom. In terms of our earlier example of the co-equal secretaries who felt free to go for a drink of water whenever they wanted, if secretary A has been told she can no longer do this and secretary B's freedom has thereby been threatened by implication, the freedom of A will be re-established by implication if secretary B proceeds to have a drink as she pleases. We might plausibly expect that when possible, one of the effects of reactance will be for a person to try to get someone else to engage in a threatened or eliminated behavior.

### The Role of Importance

As has been stated, the magnitude of reactance aroused by the loss of a given freedom is directly proportional to the importance of that freedom to the individual. But though importance therefore helps to determine the amount of reactance aroused, it does not serve in the reduction of reactance. This is because reactance is defined *not* simply as an unpleasant tension which the individual will reduce in any way that he can, such as reducing the importance of any freedom which he happens to lose, but rather as a motivational state with a specific direction, namely, the recovery of freedom. Indeed, the only reasonable expectation about the effect of reactance on the importance of a lost free behavior is that importance may increase.

### Voluntary versus Involuntary Elimination

Although the hypothetical examples used to illustrate the theory and the research to be reported all concern eliminations of freedom or threats which are involuntary, this is not meant to imply that threats and eliminations must be involuntary in order to arouse reactance. The reason that voluntary eliminations or threats have not been used in examples and research is that they involve a decision process, that is, a giving up of one or more alternatives in order to select something, which in turn would involve various conflict type and postdecisional psychological processes. While reactance theory may eventually have something of interest to say about conflict and postdecisional processes, it would seem premature to attempt such articulation here in view of the current theories which already deal with these processes (e.g., Festinger, 1957; Janis, 1959), and in view of the absence of relevant data.

## Related Concepts

The notion that people will be motivated to re-establish freedom which is threatened or eliminated is probably not new but it has not been utilized in current experimental research in psychology. For this reason we have tried to show in our examples that this theoretical formulation deals with a special set of problems and is not to be identified with various theories which deal with somewhat similar problems such as frustration, social power, etc. Nevertheless, there are theoretical concepts which are related to reactance and it may help the reader to locate the present theory if these related concepts are indicated.

While theories concerning frustration and aggression (e.g., Dollard, Doob, Miller, Mowrer, and Sears, 1939) are peripherally relevant since they deal with the blocking of goal attainment, which will sometimes also involve elimination of freedom, the most relevant concepts are those which have to do with social power. French and Raven (1959), for example, distinguish between "resisting forces" and "opposing forces" as factors which operate against positive social influence. Their definition of resisting forces as motivation instigated by the inducing force but opposite in direction is conceptually similar to the reactance formulation. However, the bases they suggest for the instigation of resisting forces are coercive measures to obtain compliance, and especially illegitimate coercion. It is only with regard to coercive inducing forces, then, that there is a close parallel between the approach of French and Raven and that of reactance theory.

Other views of social power, of course, would also tend to be relevant. For example, the analysis of power and counterpower by Thibaut and Kelly (1959) could in part be translated into terms of freedom, freedom reduction, and ways of re-establishing freedom. At the same time, one fundamental difference between their approach and reactance theory is that they do not posit a motivation to gain or recover power but rather concern themselves with the reward-cost outcomes of various kinds of power relationships.

The concepts of "personal weight" and "weight reduction" (Horwitz, 1958) seem particularly relevant and close to reactance theory. Personal weight is defined as the expected power which a person has in a given social relationship. When two people disagree, the legitimate outcome of the disagreement is a function of their weighted desires. When the actual outcome deviates from the legitimate outcome there is the implication that the disfavored member's weight has been reduced. Horwitz explicitly assumes that if the disfavored person does not redefine what is legitimate, he will generate a tension system for restoring his power to its expected level. As may be seen, this formulation is quite similar to reactance theory where personal eliminations of or threats to freedom are concerned. It is obvious, of course, that the concept of personal weight was not formulated to handle impersonal events. A second point worth noting is that while enhancement of personal weight is assumed by Horwitz to be satisfying, there is no assumption in reactance theory about reactions to increases in freedom where there has been no prior reduction.

The intention of this brief discussion of related concepts is to indicate the kinds of theoretical conceptions to which it is related, not to explore these conceptions and relationships exhaustively. While there is other relevant literature, such as Heider's (1958) discussion of "retribution," this review should suffice to locate reactance theory among previous theoretical ideas.

## Testing the Theory

It should be clear from the above presentation that reactance will frequently occur in response to restrictions or threats thereof imposed by social entities, and that the general effect of reactance is to produce tendencies to oppose the actual or threatened restrictions. That is, some kind of force is exerted upon a person and this gives rise to reactance, which may be seen as a second force opposing the first. This opposition of forces complicates the testing of the theory since it makes necessary that one somehow partial out the effects of the instigating force in order to detect the effects of reactance.

To illustrate this problem more concretely, let us imagine a person who has put a coin in a vending machine and is now trying to decide whether to take candy bar A or candy bar B. Let us further imagine that a stranger then walks up and says, "Take A." This example will be recognized as a typical social influence situation in which a "persuasive communication" has been transmitted from a communicator to a communicatee. But according to reactance theory the chooser's freedom may be threatened by the attempted social influence: the more pressure is put on the person to comply, the more his freedom not to select A and to select B is threatened. Since freedom may be re-established by selecting B (doing the opposite of what was suggested), it may be predicted that the greater is the magnitude of reactance aroused, the greater will be the chooser's tendency to select B. But with the importance of the freedom to select B held constant, the magnitude of reactance should be a direct function of the pressure to comply with the influence attempt. That is, as the pressure to comply increases, the pressure not to comply also increases and the resultant effect on the individual's final response is difficult to predict. In addition, where the magnitude of reactance is less than the pressure to comply, the individual will do what is suggested but less enthusiastically than if no reactance were experienced. Unfortunately, any decreases in the resultant strength or enthusiasm of compliance could be due to *resistance* against compliance just as well as to a *motive* against compliance, and resistance might easily occur independently of reactance. To demonstrate only resistance to compliance, then, will generally be more equivocal evidence for reactance than to demonstrate non-compliance, e.g., doing the opposite of what is suggested or "boomerang" attitude change. Thus, one general difficulty in testing for reactance effects from social pressure is that the magnitude of reactance must somehow be made greater than the pressures which give rise to the reactance.

In addition as the reader has probably noticed, the above social influence situation is nowhere nearly as simple as we have assumed. For the chooser may imagine that the attempted influence is because the communicator wants B for himself (and therefore B is better than A), or, accepting the communication as an indication that the communicator prefers A, the chooser may decide he does not want to be like someone who gives unsolicited advice and he would therefore tend to choose B. So even if it could be shown in this relatively simple situation that people would do the opposite of what was suggested to them, that in itself would not yield completely unequivocal evidence in support of reactance theory.

The problems are not altogether eliminated by testing the theory in impersonal situations. This may be seen if we recall the earlier example of the individual who wanted a pack of Camel cigarettes. In that case, after money had been placed in the vending machine, a pack of Camels was dispensed without the individual's having a chance to make his selection. Although there should be no imputation of motives or preferences to the machine, psychological processes other than reactance can still occur and obsure the effects of reactance, or make interpretation difficult. Specifically, the individual has invested his money in the machine and has been stuck with the pack of Camels regardless of any reactance he may experience. Because of his investment and the subsequent commitment to the pack of Camels, he may be resistant to derogating Camel cigarettes, as reactance would lead him to do. Similarly, if a person were about to choose one from several attractive choice alternatives and suddenly discovered that for quite impersonal reasons one was no longer available, he would be impelled by reactance to want that one even more, but at the same time, he might find it painful to want something which he clearly could not have.

In summary, the testing of reactance hypotheses is relatively complicated and difficult. Nevertheless, we hope to show in the pages which follow that not only are there interesting implications of reactance theory, but also that relatively unequivocal tests can be made.

## Summary and Plan

The theory stated in the preceding pages holds that when a person believes himself free to engage in a given behavior, he will experience psychological reactance if that freedom is eliminated or threatened with elimination. Psychological reactance is defined as a motivational state directed toward the re-establishment of the threatened or eliminated freedom, and it should manifest itself in increased desire to engage in the relevant behavior and actual attempts to engage in it. Basically, the magnitude of reactance is a direct function of (1) the importance of the freedom which is eliminated or threatened, and (2) the proportion of free behaviors eliminated or threatened.

The theoretical statement is sufficiently broad to include impersonal events, as well as personal, among those which can eliminate or threaten freedoms. It is important to demonstrate that this breadth is justified and we have therefore chosen to address this basic question before turning to implications for social processes. Chapter II therefore deals with the basic question of whether or not quite impersonal eliminations of freedom result in reactance effects. From there we proceed to a consideration of personal eliminations of freedom in Chapter III, personal threats to freedom in Chapter IV, and impersonal threats to freedom in Chapter V. Chapter VI breaks away from this scheme to give special consideration to the problem of persuasion and attitude change, an area which holds particular difficulties for application of the theory. Finally, Chapter VII summarizes the evidence and some of the lessons learned.

# CHAPTER II

# Impersonal Elimination of Freedom

The theoretical statement presented in the preceding chapter places no limit on the manner in which an elimination of freedom takes place: reactance will be aroused to the extent that the eliminated freedom has importance to the individual. That reactance arousal and its effects are so general may not be obvious and for this reason it is important to demonstrate that reactance effects occur with completely impersonal eliminations of freedom. This chapter, then, will indicate how impersonal eliminations of freedom can occur, what the consequent reactance effects may be, and, finally, evidence that reactance effects do in fact occur when impersonal eliminations of freedom take place.

The significant aspect of an *impersonal* elimination (or threat) is that an individual cannot easily perceive it as having been *directed* at himself. Rather, his loss of freedom could just as well have happened to someone else. That is, the elimination of his freedom is at least in part fortuitous and occurred only because of some set of circumstances which has nothing to do with him, personally. For example, the individual might notice, while shopping at a supermarket, that the particular kind of coffee he sometimes buys is out of stock. That other people have bought this kind of coffee and that the supermarket did not have a larger supply could hardly have been done in order to eliminate his freedom and he will not be likely to think that this elimination of his freedom was directed at him personally.

Unless an impersonal elimination is justified—i.e., explained as due to an unusual set of circumstances—it can sometimes carry the implication of future threats to one's freedoms. For in the absence of having some reason for the elimination, it will frequently be possible for the individual to imagine that other eliminations will also tend to occur. Thus, in the above supermarket example, unless the individual can learn that there was an unusually heavy run on his particular brand of coffee or that the supplier's deliveryman was ill, he can easily think that his coffee will frequently be out of stock or that other items in the store may go out of stock. These implied further eliminations of freedom would, of course, increase the amount of reactance he would experience.

An elimination, as opposed to a threat of elimination, means that the freedom in question is irrevocably lost. There is neither the possibility of avoiding nor recovering the freedom in question. The most obvious theoretical implication is that when a freedom is eliminated, the individual will be unable to re-establish it directly by engaging in the relevant behavior. Nevertheless, the motivational state of reactance should occur and would result in increased desire to participate in the relevant behavior.

It should be clear from the above discussion that an impersonal elimination of freedom would provide a relatively simple and sound test of the theory. Because the elimination is impersonal, the individual is unlikely to impute motives for it and then to respond to the motives which he has imputed. With imputed motives made unlikely, the individual's response can more confidently be attributed to reactance. What is needed is a test of the following proposition: *if a specific behavioral freedom of a person is eliminated by impersonal events, he will experience reactance and consequently will see increased attractiveness in the eliminated behavior.*

A situation which lends itself to the testing of this proposition is that in which a person is about to select one of several attractive choice alternatives. We turn, therefore, to a brief analysis of the predecisional situation.

When a person has two or more alternatives to choose from, it is implied that he is free to select any one. Thus, where the alternatives are A, B, and C, his set of free behaviors in the predecisional situation consists of selecting A, selecting B, and selecting C. In order to simplify the analysis, let us assume that the alternatives are clearly attractive, and let us ignore the further free behaviors of not selecting the alternatives. The importance of any of these free behaviors (to select A, B, and C) is dependent upon their having potential for satisfying *different* needs, i.e., items A, B, and C must differ from each other qualitatively. If they were identical-looking oranges, for example, the importance of being free to select A would be reduced by having the freedom to select B or C, which have the same potential for satisfaction of the same need. It should be noted in this connection that object attractiveness, which implies potential need satisfaction is a necessary but not sufficient condition for importance of freedom.

Given that the choice alternatives would satisfy different needs, the importance of being able to choose a given alternative is a direct function of its absolute level of attractiveness and of its attractiveness relative to the other choice alternatives. When relative attractiveness of the alternatives is held constant, the greater is the absolute attractiveness of a given alternative, the greater will be the importance of the freedom to select it. When the absolute attractiveness of a given alternative is held constant, the higher is its relative attractiveness compared to other alternatives, the greater will be the importance of the freedom to select it.

It follows that when a person is about to select one from several choice alternatives which are attractive and differ from each other qualitatively, the elimination of one alternative will arouse reactance. The magnitude of this reactance will be a direct function of the absolute and relative attractiveness of the alternative lost. Therefore, the greater is the absolute and/or relative attractiveness of a choice alternative which is eliminated, the greater will be its apparent increase in attractiveness.

With the absolute level of an alternative's attractiveness held constant, and other things being equal, the maximum amount of reactance which can be created by its elimination will occur when it is the most attractive of the available alternatives. This consideration implies that an experimental test would most clearly demonstrate reactance effects if the most attractive of a person's choice alternatives were eliminated. Experimentally, however, there is a danger in this procedure in that the individual would inevitably be in a condition of frustration as well as reactance arousal.

It is conceivable that frustration would result in increased attractiveness of the goal object. In order to make sure frustration does not occur so as to eliminate this frustration-attraction view as an alternative explanation, the choice alternative to be restricted must not be the most attractive one. Furthermore, since there will be some imprecision in an experimental situation in determining which alternative is most attractive, which next most, etc., to eliminate the "second most attractive alternative" may also occasionally frustrate a person since it will sometimes be what he intended to select. It is for this reason that in the first two experiments to be reported, the third most attractive of four alternatives was picked for the experimentally contrived elimination.

The elimination of the third most attractive choice alternative is a very difficult test for reactance theory. For in addition to its absolute attractiveness being somewhat lower than that of the first and second alternatives, its *relative* attractiveness is quite low, and the resultant importance of being free to choose it cannot be very great. Nevertheless, it was felt that the value of clearly ruling out the possible operation of frustration was sufficiently great to warrant the danger of not obtaining strong reactance effects.

An experimental test of the proposition that the elimination of a choice alternative will result in increased attractiveness of that alternative can be arranged quite easily. It is simply required that a person be given the impression he will be allowed to choose one of four attractive items, that he rate them on attractiveness, that prior to his making a selection he learn that one alternative is unavailable, and that he then rate them again. This was the basic model for two experiments reported by Brehm, Stires, Sensenig, and Shaban (1966).

The first experiment was designed to show that an eliminated choice alternative becomes more attractive, and that this effect increases as the absolute attractiveness of the choice alternatives increases. The procedure was as follows.

The subjects were students from an introductory psychology course who volunteered to participate in a two-session "Market Analysis of Phonograph Records." When a student arrived for his experimental session, he was told that the psychology department had received a contract from a company which distributed phonograph records to obtain judgments about some recorded selections which might be of interest to college students. The selections were taped recordings of folk music. It was explained to the subject that he would listen to the selections in order to indicate how much he liked each one, and that he would be asked to perform a similar task during his second session, the following day.

At this point the experimenter announced that the distributing company wanted each participant to have a complimentary record for his help on the study, and that he was hopeful that the shipment of complimentary records would arrive the following morning. The manipulation of attractiveness of the choice alternatives was introduced by the experimenter's telling some subjects that the gift records were 45 rpm singles (worth about $1 each) and other subjects that the records were the long-play (LP) albums (worth about $3 each) from which the single selections were taken. Thus, the subject was led to believe that he would be able to choose any one of the four either 45 rpm or LP records as a reward for his participation.

After filling out a brief questionnaire on his music listening habits and preferences, the subject listened to each of the four selections, rating each on a "0" to "100" scale of favorability immediately after listening to it. The subjects were then scheduled for a second session and excused.

At the start of the second session the subject was informed he would hear the same four selections and rate them again in order to see if hearing a record a second time might affect one's evaluation of it. The experimenter then said that the shipment of complimentary records had arrived that morning, but that the shipment, for some unknown reason, had failed to include copies of one of the four records. This unavailable record was identified as that which the subject had rated third most favorable on the previous day. Care was taken to avoid the implication that this record was unavailable because of greater popularity. Finally, subjects listened to the four selections and rated them again, they were interviewed briefly in order to detect any suspicions about the experimental procedure, and the purposes and deceptions of the experiment were revealed and explained.

In summary, subjects were given the impression they would be able to choose a 45 rpm (Low Attractiveness) or LP (High Attractiveness) record on the basis of the four selections which they heard and rated on two different occasions. Prior to the second rating, however, they were informed that the record whose selection they had initially rated third most attractive had not been included in the shipment of complimentary records and was therefore unavailable. In addition to these experimental conditions, control conditions were run, using both 45 rpm and LP choice alternatives, in which everything was the same as in the experimental conditions except that there was no elimination of a choice alternative.

It was expected that the eliminated alternative would tend to increase in attractiveness, and that this increase would be greater where the choice alternatives were LP records than where they were 45 rpm records. As it turned out, however, this attempt to manipulate the attractiveness of the choice alternatives failed to have any effect on changes in attractiveness of the eliminated record. Because of this failure, which will be discussed later, and in order to simplify the presentation, the results of the Low and High Attractiveness conditions are combined into single Control and Elimination conditions.

The initial attractiveness ratings of the four records (Table I) show that there was a slight tendency for attractiveness to be somewhat higher in the Elimination condition, especially for the critical rank 3 record, although none of these differences approaches statistical reliability. In any case, if there were any tendency for the rank 3 record to rise to the mean value of the other records, that tendency would be greater in the Control condition since it has the lower initial score.

TABLE I

INITIAL ATTRACTIVENESS RATINGS OF THE 4 RECORDS

|  | Initial rank of record | | | |
| --- | --- | --- | --- | --- |
|  | 1 | 2 | 3 | 4 |
| Control ($N = 14$) | 84.1[a] | 73.6 | 50.9 | 36.3 |
| Elimination ($N = 33$) | 86.7 | 77.6 | 59.7 | 38.5 |

[a] 100 = high attractiveness.

Table II presents changes in attractiveness of the rank 3 record and, for comparison, the combined mean change of the other three records. The difference in change in attractiveness of the rank 3 record is as predicted, with the Elimination condition showing a clear increase (greater than no change at the 1% level, $t = 2.89$, $df = 32$),[1] and the Control showing essentially no change at all. However, apparently because of the small $N$ in the Control condition, the difference between Elimination and Control conditions fails to reach an acceptable level of significance ($t = 1.38$).

A tabulation of persons who showed increased attractiveness ratings, no change, or decreased ratings yields the same picture.

[1] All $p$ values are two-tailed unless specified otherwise.

TABLE II

CHANGE IN ATTRACTIVENESS RATINGS

| | Rank 3 record | Other records |
|---|---|---|
| Control | $.32^a$ | 3.04 |
| Elimination | 6.33 | 1.08 |

[a] Positive change indicates increased attractiveness.

These data, shown in Table III, also fail to yield an acceptable significance level for the difference between conditions ($x^2 = 2.60$, $p = .11$, with No Changers omitted). However, they show a significant tendency on the part of subjects in the Elimination condition to raise their rating ($x^2 = 7.50$, $p < .01$) and no dominant tendency among Control subjects either to raise or lower their rating of the rank 3 record. Thus, while both mean change and frequency data failed to show a statistically significant difference between the Control and Elimination conditions, they were consistent with our expectations that there would be little or no change in the Control condition and an increase in attractiveness in the Elimination condition.

The failure of the manipulation of attractiveness to have its expected effect on the magnitude of the increased attraction of the restricted alternative is not difficult to understand. First, because the rationale of the study called for unfamiliar selections of music, it proved impossible to find four highly attractive ones. The initial ratings of the third and fourth records therefore tended to be quite low—around 55 (on the 100 point scale) for the third, and around 37 for the fourth. These ratings, which are 20 to nearly 40 points below

TABLE III

FREQUENCY OF INCREASED, DECREASED, AND UNCHANGED ATTRACTIVENESS
RATINGS OF THE RANK 3 RECORD

| | Attraction change | | |
|---|---|---|---|
| | Increase | No change | Decrease |
| Control | 6 | 1 | 7 |
| Elimination | 23 | 3 | 7 |

that for the second-rated record, indicate that the restricted record was not very attractive. Since the LP album, the presumably high attraction choice item, had to be judged by the single selection which the subject heard, it could only have been judged as not very attractive. If a person does not care much for oatmeal, a gallon of it is certainly not more attractive than a bowl of it. In short, the manipulation of attractiveness failed apparently because the third-rated selection was not sufficiently attractive to make more of the same thing more attractive.

Because the attractiveness manipulation failed, the increased attractiveness of the eliminated record is more easily attributable to factors other than reactance. For example, the experimenter's having mentioned this record may have led to more reconsideration of it and consequent increased liking. Second, although the experimenter tried to avoid any implication that the record was unavailable because it was more popular, subjects may still have made this inference and therefore raised their own appraisal. Third, the fact that the record was unavailable may have produced less reconsideration of it and thereby less restraint against a regression tendency for the rating of initially low-rated items to increase. And fourth, it is possible that under the conditions of the experiment, a person wants what he cannot have regardless of whether or not the elimination reduces his freedom. That is, even if one were not free to choose for himself, the elimination of a possible gift item may make that item more attractive.

In order to eliminate these ambiguities of interpretation and strengthen the difference between the Elimination and Control conditions, a second experiment was designed and carried out. The design of this second study was arranged to replicate the increase in attractiveness of an eliminated choice alternative and to show that the increased attraction occurs only when the elimination also reduces the individual's freedom.

The basic procedure and design were the same, except that there was no attempt to manipulate attractiveness of choice alternatives, and a condition was added in which subjects were never given the freedom to choose which record they would receive. In this new condition, however, the third-rated record was eliminated in precisely the same way as in the choice condition, thus holding constant the factors of drawing attention to it and making it unavailable.

In order to insure that the less attractive records would still be quite attractive, relatively well-known recordings were selected through pilot work, and all subjects were promised an LP album as a reward for returning for the second session. In the first session, subjects in the Choice conditions, as before, were told they would be able to choose any of the four LP albums from which the four selections they were to hear had come. In the No Choice condition, subjects were told that because there was a limited number of records, the records would be given out randomly and that each person would receive one of the four records. Otherwise, the first session was essentially the same as before: subjects listened to the four selections and rated the attractiveness of each.

At the beginning of the second session, subjects in the Choice condition were reminded that at the end of the day's session they would be able to choose one of the records for themselves. Those in the No Choice condition were reminded that the records were being distributed randomly and were told that at the end of the day's session they would draw a slip from a box to determine which record they would receive. The elimination of the third-rated record, as in the first experiment, was carried out by telling subjects that the shipment of records had failed to include that particular record.

Thus, in this second experiment, there was a condition in which subjects had the impression they would be able to choose any of the four records, there was a second condition in which subjects had the impression they would be able to choose any of the four records and then learned that the third-rated record was unavailable, and there was a third condition in which subjects were under the impression they would receive one of the four records, selected at random, and then learned that the third-rated record was unavailable.

The initial attractiveness scores, shown in Table IV, indicate that the attempt to obtain more equally attractive records was successful, since the relative ratings of the rank 3 and rank 4 records are higher than in the first experiment. These ratings also show that there is essentially no difference between conditions in initial ratings.

It was expected that the attractiveness of the rank 3 record would show little or no change in the Choice – No Elimination condition, but that in the Choice – Elimination condition it would increase, this being the pattern predicted, and observed in the first experiment. This expectation is supported by the attraction change scores, presented

TABLE IV

INITIAL ATTRACTIVENESS RATINGS OF THE 4 RECORDS

|  | Initial rank of record | | | |
|---|---|---|---|---|
|  | 1 | 2 | 3 | 4 |
| Choice – No Elimination ($N = 14$) | 85.8[a] | 76.6 | 66.3 | 53.8 |
| Choice – Elimination ($N = 13$) | 86.8 | 78.2 | 69.2 | 57.4 |
| No Choice – Elimination ($N = 15$) | 90.9 | 81.9 | 73.0 | 64.3 |

[a] $100$ = high attractiveness.

TABLE V

CHANGE IN ATTRACTIVENESS RATINGS

|  | Rank 3 record | Other records |
|---|---|---|
| Choice – No Elimination | .07[a] | −.64 |
| Choice – Elimination | 4.23 | −.46 |
| No Choice – Elimination | −5.40 | −.93 |

[a] Positive change indicates increased attractiveness.

in Table V. The difference between the Choice – Elimination and No Elimination conditions is not statistically reliable but these data may be combined with those of the Elimination and Control conditions of the previous experiment to yield an overall estimate of the reliability of this effect. The resultant increase in attractiveness for the combined Choice – Elimination conditions (5.74) is then found to be greater than the change in the combined Choice – No Elimination conditions (.20) at the 9% level ($t = 1.74$, $df = 72$). Furthermore, a tabulation for the combined experiments of those who increased, did not change, or decreased their rating of the rank 3 record, as seen in Table VI, shows that the difference between the Choice – Elimination and No Elimination conditions (omitting those who did not change) is significant at the 5% level ($\chi^2 = 4.07$). For the combined results, both mean change and frequency data indicate there is no dominant tendency among Choice – No Elimination subjects either to raise or lower their ratings

TABLE VI

FREQUENCY OF INCREASED, DECREASED, AND UNCHANGED ATTRACTIVENESS
RATINGS OF THE RANK 3 RECORD FOR THE TWO EXPERIMENTS COMBINED

| | Attraction change | | |
| --- | --- | --- | --- |
| | Increase | No change | Decrease |
| Choice – No Elimination | 12 | 3 | 13 |
| Choice – Elimination | 31 | 5 | 10 |

of the rank 3 record, while there is a clear tendency among Choice – Elimination subjects to raise their rating ($p < .005$ by either $t$ or $\chi^2$). The combined results indicate, then, that when the rank 3 record is eliminated, it does in fact tend to become more attractive.

We may now turn to the second concern of the present experiment, namely, the question of whether or not prior freedom to choose the eliminated alternative is a necessary condition for the resultant increase in attractiveness. Table V shows that the attractiveness of the rank 3 record in the No Choice – Elimination condition decreased ($-5.40$). This decrease is significantly different from the increase in the Choice – Elimination condition (4.23) at the 3% level ($t = 2.43$, $df = 26$). Evidently, then, and in line with the theory, prior freedom to choose the alternative accounts for its increase in attractiveness when it is eliminated. Furthermore, the data clearly fail to support the alternative hypotheses that increased salience of the alternative due to its being eliminated, or the elimination per se, will tend to result in increased attractiveness ratings.

Postexperimental questionnaire data were consistent with the rating changes. For example, subjects were asked to indicate which record they most wanted for their gift, which next most, etc. The rankings of the initially third-rated record are shown in Table VII, where it can be seen that there is no effect in the Choice – No Elimination condition, a relatively high ranking in the Choice – Elimination condition, and a relatively low ranking in the No Choice – Elimination condition.

It was intended by the design that subjects not be frustrated by the elimination procedure, and for this reason, the third-rated record was the one eliminated. Some evidence on the success of this arrangement

TABLE VII

RANKING OF THE THIRD-RATED RECORD AS GIFT FOR SELF

|  | Rank | | |
| --- | --- | --- | --- |
|  | 1 or 2[a] | 3 | 4 |
| Choice – No Elimination | 6 | 3 | 5 |
| Choice – Elimination | 8 | 4 | 1 |
| No Choice – Elimination | 1 | 7 | 7 |

[a] A rank of 1 was given by one subject in Choice – No Elimination and by two subjects in Choice – Elimination.

is available from postexperimental questionnaire data. A question which asked subjects to check possible reasons for disappointment or annoyance at the restriction included the following two responses:

"because I definitely wanted this record as my free gift."

"because I thought I might have wanted this record as my free gift." Neither response was checked by any subject in either restriction condition. We may conclude that the attempt to avoid frustration was successful.

Finally, it is of interest to consider the nature of the elimination itself. The failure of the record to be included in the shipment was essentially a fortuitous event, completely impersonal from the subject's point of view. In both experiments the experimenter put on an apologetic air when giving these instructions, and in the second experiment, explicitly apologized for the failure. Thus, there was an attempt to minimize any hostile feelings the subject may have felt toward the experiment or experimenter. In effect, the elimination of the alternative was made to look like one of those completely impersonal things that "just happens". The significant point of this is that the arousal of reactance does not depend upon social restriction or threat, but rather upon the loss of freedom per se, for whatever reasons.

Let us turn now to another demonstration of the effects of elimination of freedom. As will be seen, this second demonstration concerns another basic proposition of the reactance formulation and also serves as a conceptual replication of the experiments just reported.

## The Proportion of Freedom Eliminated

The magnitude of reactance is a direct function of the proportion of free behaviors eliminated or threatened with elimination. However, with the set of free behaviors held constant, the greater is the number eliminated, the greater is the number over which the effects of reactance will be spread. Thus, one could not safely say that for a given eliminated free behavior there would be greater reactance effects, such as an increase in attractiveness, as the number of eliminated free behaviors increased. To determine that the total amount of reactance effects increased with an increase in the number of freedoms eliminated would require some rather elaborate rules for combining different reactance effects and would be, in any case, somewhat trivial.

There is, however, another form of the general proposition which is capable of a relatively clear test and thereby of providing further evidence relevant to the theory. According to this form, with the elimination or threat of elimination of a specific free behavior, the greater is the number of behaviors in the free set, the less will be the magnitude of reactance. In this case, the effects of reactance are focused on a single behavior so that comparison measurements can be relatively clear. The hypothesis, then, is that when a given free behavior is eliminated, the smaller is the number of available free behaviors, the greater will be the magnitude of reactance and consequent increase in desire for the eliminated behavior.

Since this hypothesis may be considered an elaboration of that tested by the previous two experiments, it, too, may conveniently be tested in a choice situation. The number of behavioral freedoms available to a person can be established by giving him greater or lesser numbers of choice alternatives. Of course, in line with the previous analysis of the predecisional situation, the choice alternatives must be useful for the satisfaction of different potentially important needs. Furthermore, in order to create a significant amount of reactance, the one eliminated must be relatively (and absolutely) attractive. It is also necessary to hold constant the absolute and relative attractiveness of the eliminated alternative, and this may be accomplished by making available to the individual, for example, a set of six alternatives in one condition, and the top three of the same six alternatives in the other conditions. Thus, the elimination of any of the top three alternatives would be possible without changing either absolute or relative (to the top three) attractiveness. Finally, as in the previous two experiments, it is possible to avoid any interpretation in terms of frustration by eliminating an alternative other than the most attractive one.

Two experiments along these lines were carried out by myself, Dorothy McQuown, and Janet Shaban. Both experiments used the same procedure, but since the results of the first experiment[2] were simply suggestive, we will not describe it in detail. Briefly, then, subjects rated and ranked their desire to see each of six movies from short descriptions of them, were led to believe that they would be able to choose one of all six to see, or that they would be able to choose one of their top three, and some of each of these groups were then informed that their third-ranked movie had been damaged in shipment and would be unavailable. Subsequent ratings and rankings, taken prior to the choice, provided a measure of change in desire to see the third-ranked movie. The results showed that while the ratings and rankings changed very little in the conditions without any elimination, they tended to go down in conditions with elimination. But the decrease in desire to see the eliminated movie was reliably less in the condition with three alternatives than in the condition with six. Thus, it seemed possible that for some reason there was a general tendency in this experiment to see the eliminated movie as less desirable, and that this tendency overwhelmed the slight amount of reactance in the six alternative conditions, resulting in a large decrease in desire. This is, perhaps, not too surprising since a similar effect was seen in the No Choice – Elimination condition of the previously described experiment by Brehm, Stires, Sensenig, and Shaban. However, in the three alternative conditions, in which the magnitude of reactance should have been greater, the reactance effect of increased desire and the opposing effect of decreased desire apparently canceled each other out, resulting in a slight decrease in desire to see the eliminated movie.

While other interpretations of these results were possible, it seemed worthwhile to conduct a partial replication in which, in addition, the effect of prior freedom could be examined. Therefore, in addition to conditions in which subjects were led to believe they could choose from either three or six alternatives, the second experiment included conditions in which subjects were led to believe they would be randomly

[2] McQuown, Dorothy, "Changes in the attractiveness of a restricted alternative when the total number of alternatives is varied." Unpublished Senior Honors Thesis, Duke University, 1964.

assigned to one of either three or six alternatives. It was expected that where subjects were assigned, and therefore had no freedom, the desire to have the eliminated alternative would show little or no increase nor would it increase more when there were three alternatives than when there were six. Also, in order to increase the importance of the eliminated freedom, the second-ranked alternative was eliminated instead of the third. A final change which should be noted is that instead of attributing the loss of the movie to damage in shipment, it was said that one movie failed to be included in the shipment of movies. This change was made because of the possibility that some subjects in the first experiment may have marked the restricted movie down because it was damaged—i.e., one does not want to see a damaged movie.

## METHOD

The general plan again was to have students indicate how much they would like to see each of six different movies as judged from descriptions of them, to give them a choice from all six or from their top three and subsequently eliminate the second-ranked alternative, and finally to have them again indicate how much they would like to see each movie. Subjects in conditions without prior freedom were also told they would see one of six or one of three movies, but they were informed that they would be assigned to a movie by chance rather than by choice. In order to assess the absolute change in attraction to the eliminated movie in the condition of highest reactance (choice of three alternatives), some subjects were given a choice of three alternatives with no subsequent elimination of the one ranked second.

### Premeasure

The experimenter and an assistant entered all eighth-grade classrooms of a single school during regular school hours, were introduced as being from Duke University, and immediately passed out questionnaires to the students. The experimenter announced that she was working for a (fictitious) national educational organization, and that she was presently testing a series of movies which were designed both to be enjoyable and to have educational value. She explained that the students could help in her testing program by filling out the questionnaires they had been given and she gave instructions for completing the questionnaire. The students were asked not to talk either while filling out the questionnaire or afterward since the experimenter might return in a few days to ask more questions about the movies, and she was, she said, particularly desirous of finding out how each one personally felt about the movies. The experimenter said their names were needed only so she could tell who filled out a questionnaire and who had not, and that their answers would never be seen by any of the teachers or other students. When the questionnaires were completed, the subjects were again cautioned not to talk and were thanked for their help. Care was taken to avoid any implication that movies would actually be shown.

### Questionnaires

The premeasure questionnaire gave a brief description of each of six different (fictitious) movies, e.g., "*The Brave Bulls*—Not only does this film have the glamour and excitement of the bullring, but it also tells the fascinating story of Mexico's most famous bull fighter." Each of the six movie descriptions was accompanied by the question, "How much would you like to see this movie?" and a seven-point rating scale running from "Not at all" to "Very very much." At the end of the questionnaire was a rank scale on which the subject was to write in which movie he would most like to see, which next most, etc.

Before the second session, subjects who completed the premeasure questionnaire were randomly assigned to conditions and an experimental booklet was prepared for each. The booklet consisted of a cover page containing only the subject's name, a second page containing a list of all six movies (Six-alternative condition) or his top three movies (Three-alternative condition) arranged from most to least preferred according to the subject's own rank ordering, and, finally, a questionnaire identical to that used for the premeasure.

### Experimental Session

All subjects assigned to a given condition were sent to the same room and remained there for the period of time necessary to run all second-session conditions. It was explained by the teachers of these groups that there was to be some kind of special testing that day and that the eighth-grade students had been divided into different groups depending upon their age. The experimenter and assistant visited one group after another, subjecting each group to a different set of conditions.

In each condition subjects were first given their experimental booklets, and the experimenter reminded them that she was trying to find out how much they liked movies which were supposed to be both entertaining and educational. She then announced that she had just found out she would be able to show each student a movie sometime during the coming week. In *Choice* conditions the experimenter said, "If you'll look on the second page of the questionnaire I've given you, you'll see stapled there the list of movies you can choose from. These are the ones we have available, and you can see any one of them you like, but before you make a decision on one, I want to show you some photographs taken from these movies to help you make up your mind."

In *No Choice* conditions the experimenter said, "If you'll look on the second page of the questionnaire I've given you, you'll see stapled there the list of movies you might see. Each of you will be assigned to one of the movies on the list, but just which one you'll see hasn't been decided yet. We will decide that later by drawing names. And before we draw names to see who will see which movie, we're also going to show you some photographs from each movie so that you'll have a better idea of what each movie is like."

In both Choice and No Choice conditions, the experimenter then asked the subjects to fill out the rating and ranking questionnaire since "Sometimes a person's opinion changes over a few days and I want to see if that has happened here." In the single condition with *No Elimination* of an alternative, subjects were allowed to complete the questionnaire at this point. However, in the four conditions with *Elimination* of an alternative, before subjects could start to work on the questionnaire, an assistant entered the room and whispered to the experimenter, who then turned to the subjects and announced that " . . . one of the movies did not arrive with the others, so you will not be able to see that movie." The experimenter and assistant then circulated among the subjects in order to mark the second-ranked movie off each one's list. Subjects were told to rate all six movies on the questionnaire anyway and were then allowed to complete the questionnaire.

The subjects in each condition were questioned immediately upon completion of the experiment in order to discover any marked suspicion or irregularities which might affect the outcome. A procedural problem which developed in one condition is noted below. The subjects were finally given a complete explanation of the deceptions, etc., and were all provided with a free pass to a local movie theater.

## Subjects and Design

Subjects were 163 eighth-grade students from Jordan Junior High School in Durham, North Carolina[3] who attended both the premeasure and experimental sessions. All students who filled out the prequestion-naire were randomly assigned to one of the five conditions: Three Alternatives, Choice, No Elimination (to be called Control); Three Alternatives, Choice, Elimination (Three Alternative – Choice); Six Alternatives, Choice, Elimination (Six Alternative – Choice); Three Alternatives, No Choice, Elimination (Three Alternative – No Choice); and Six Alternatives, No Choice, Elimination (Six Alter-native – No Choice).

While the four Elimination groups were intended to be about equal in size, absences and irregularities in the second session or question-naire responses reduced the two No Choice conditions to somewhat smaller sizes. In particular, some of the subjects in the Six Alternative – No Choice condition had to be seated around tables where it proved impossible to keep them from seeing each others' lists of movies and from learning that not everyone had the same movie marked off his list. The data from these nine subjects were deleted prior to analysis. Eight subjects from the other conditions were omitted due to incom-plete second questionnaires.

## RESULTS

Let us briefly review our expectations for this experiment. Among subjects given choice, there should be an increase in desire to see the eliminated movie, and this increase should be greater among those who had three choice alternatives than among those who had six. For

[3] For all of their help and cooperation, the investigators wish to express their appreciation to Mr. A. E. Ashe, Principal of Hillandale School, and the eighth-grade teachers there including Miss Sandra Boger, Mrs. Susan Hatcher, and Mr. W. M. McCauley, and to Mr. A. H. Best, Principal of Holt School, and the eighth-grade teachers there including Mrs. Beulah Timblin, Mrs. Betty Whitfield, and Mr. Charles Winchester, and to Mr. John T. Smith, Principal of Jordan Junior-Senior High School, and the eighth-grade teachers there including Mrs. Jere Blackburn, Mrs. Juanita Campbell, Mrs. Ann Crawford, Mrs. Joyce Burkhardt, Mrs. Rebecca Pipkin, Mrs. Myrna Fisher, and Mrs. Sarah Sheaffer.

subjects without choice there should be no increase in desire to see the eliminated alternative regardless of the number of alternatives involved.

The mean rating changes in desire to see the second-ranked movie supported the expected pattern. Only in the three alternative condition with choice was the mean decrease in desire (− .18) less than the decrease in the Control (− .40). Furthermore, the difference between mean changes in the conditions with three and six alternatives was greater where there was choice (.43) than where there was no choice (.17). However, none of these differences was statistically reliable.

A frequency count of the direction of rating change proved to be more supportive. This analysis, shown in Table VIII, indicates a trend for subjects in the Three Alternative – Choice condition to raise their rating of the eliminated alternative, while subjects in all other conditions show either no change or a slight tendency to decrease their ratings. The Three Alternative – Choice condition is reliably different from the Six Alternative – Choice condition ($\chi^2$ with $2df = 10.82$, $p < .01$), from the Three Alternative – No Choice condition ($\chi^2$ with $2\ df = 6.17$, $p < .05$), and approaches being reliably different from the Control ($\chi^2$ with $2\ df = 4.61$, $p = .10$). The rank change measure yielded similar results except that the only reliable difference was between Three-Alternative and Six-Alternative conditions for those who had choice: there was a greater tendency to rank the eliminated alternative higher among those who had three alternatives than among those who had six ($\chi^2$ with $2\ df = 6.61$, $p < .05$).

TABLE VIII

NUMBER OF SUBJECTS SHOWING HIGHER, EQUAL, OR LOWER DESIRABILITY
RATINGS OF THE INITIALLY SECOND-RANKED MOVIE[a]

|  | Higher | Equal | Lower |
|---|---|---|---|
| Choice |  |  |  |
| Control | 5 | 8 | 5 |
| 6 Alternatives | 2 | 11 | 6 |
| 3 Alternatives | 9 | 2 | 5 |
| No Choice |  |  |  |
| 6 Alternatives | 1 | 8 | 2 |
| 3 Alternatives | 3 | 7 | 3 |

[a] Subjects whose initial rating of the rank 2 movie was at the top of the scale are omitted since their ratings could not increase.

These results support two propositions: (1) the elimination of a choice alternative arouses reactance and a consequent increased desire to have the eliminated alternative; and (2) given the elimination of a choice alternative, the magnitude of reactance and consequent increased desire for the eliminated alternative is inversely proportional to the number of choice alternatives available.

Before we leave these experiments on the elimination of a choice alternative, let us attempt to put them in some perspective. It will be recalled that all four experiments were designed to minimize the possibility of frustrating subjects, and the cost of this safeguard was a theoretical reduction in the magnitude of reactance effects which could be expected. But the predicted effects do occur, even under these difficult conditions, and they appear to be fairly consistent over different experiments. It is this consistency despite the difficulties which lends rather strong support for the theory.

The results of these studies have also suggested a complicating factor in the present formulation. In two of the four experiments, there was a rather clear tendency for subjects in low reactance conditions to show a decrease in attraction to the eliminated alternative. While this effect is not entirely unexpected, we have no theoretical explanation for it and cannot be completely clear about how it relates to reactance theory. We would assume, however, that it is a general tendency to derogate whatever one might have had but for some reason now cannot have—i.e., a "sour grapes" effect. This implies that the "sour grapes" effect is likely to occur whenever there is a behavioral elimination (not necessarily a free behavior), and that it will tend to subtract from reactance effects. Ultimately, then, the "sour grapes" effect must be clarified theoretically in order to have better understanding of the operation of reactance from the loss of a behavioral freedom.

The experiments reported here utilized a choice situation to test the assertion that reactance results from the irrevocable loss of a freedom. This was because the choice situation lends itself to the desired conditions and provides a relevant dependent variable, attractiveness of, or desire for, the choice alternatives. Theoretically, a wide variety of situations which do not involve explicit choice alternatives but nevertheless impersonally eliminate a freedom could also give rise to reactance and would lend themselves to testing of the theory.

## Summary

In this chapter we have concerned ourselves with the general proposition that an irrevocable loss of a behavioral freedom results in reactance. The predecisional aspect of a choice situation was then analyzed and shown to lend itself to a test of the general proposition. The specific hypothesis first considered was that the elimination of a choice alternative arouses reactance and a consequent increase in the attractiveness of that alternative. Two experiments in support of this hypothesis were described. A secondary hypothesis, that the magnitude of reactance would vary directly with the attractiveness of the choice alternatives, was not supported, apparently because of a methodological failure.

Two further experiments were then described which were designed to test the proposition that the magnitude of reactance is a direct function of the proportion of free behaviors eliminated. The specific hypothesis was that the magnitude of reactance and consequent increase in desire to have an eliminated choice alternative is inversely related to the number of choice alternatives available. This hypothesis was supported by the results.

Finally, it was noted that there was consistent support for the reactance hypotheses despite the design which avoided frustration but also reduced the theoretically expected magnitude of reactance. Furthermore, a "sour grapes" effect was noted in some of the results, which also presumably mitigated the reactance effects. A better understanding of the "sour grapes" effect will facilitate the testing of reactance hypotheses.

# CHAPTER III

# Personal Elimination of Freedom

Since we have seen in the preceding chapter that an impersonal elimination of a behavioral freedom results in increased attractiveness of the eliminated behavior, let us turn to an analysis of the somewhat more complicated problem of personal elimination of freedom. We may speak of a personal elimination when one of a person's free behaviors is eliminated and he can perceive or easily imagine that the elimination was intentionally aimed at him. Of course, intention will sometimes be attributed to infrahuman animals and to inanimate nature. This makes our definition of personal elimination somewhat broad and vague, but it will nevertheless serve as a guideline for the following discussion. For our concern in this chapter is with the situational factors which will normally be involved in determining the arousal and magnitude of reactance when one's freedom has been apparently purposely reduced by another person or organization, and with the possible and likely effects of reactance in these circumstances.

Personal elimination of freedom occurs in at least two distinguishable ways. First, a behavioral freedom may be eliminated by a person or organization which has considerable power over one. The individual is literally forced, either physically or through threats of relatively great punishment or loss of reward, to give up a behavioral freedom. Typical relationships which would make possible the personal elimination of freedom through exertion of power are employer-employee, parent-child, and guard-prisoner.

However, for a social agent to have power over one and to attempt to use it is not enough to produce an elimination of freedom. It is only if that agent can and will survey one's behavior relatively constantly that elimination is sure to take place. Of course, if the penalty for engaging in a given behavior which has been "eliminated" is rather severe, then less surveillance will be needed to produce actual elimination than if the penalty is rather mild. That is, we may expect the individual to weigh the likelihood of getting caught along with the penalty that goes with it. If, having assessed these factors, the individual considers engaging in the behavior to be out of the question, then it has been effectively eliminated even though it is still objectively possible. This is, of course, why we would refer to an *elimination* of freedom rather than to a *threat* of elimination.

The second way in which personal elimination of a free behavior can occur is by an irreversible act performed by someone of relatively low social power. Normally, of course, since the individual has relatively high power over the perpetrator, he would prevent the elimination if he only knew that it would occur. The point is that one cannot predict the behavior of others perfectly, nor can one always keep surveillance over others when they are unpredictable and capable of performing some act which will eliminate a freedom. At the same time, the only way that someone of relatively low power can eliminate a freedom of an individual is by having access to things and events necessary to that freedom. Consider, for example, the books and journals which a professor keeps in his office to maintain his freedom to refer to relevant literature. If the professor kept this material locked up, then this freedom to refer to literature could not be reduced or eliminated by someone's taking a book when the professor had stepped out of his office. But if he does not keep this material locked up, then his freedom to refer to book X can be eliminated by someone's taking book X. Of course, not everyone has access to taking a book. It is those people who go into his office for one reason or another who have access, and by and large, these will be students, colleagues, secretaries, service personnel, etc. In general, those who have access to the things and events which are necessary to one's freedoms are friends, colleagues, family members, and people who offer services. While all of the eliminations of freedom by members of these groups will not be seen as intentional, many will be and therefore constitute personal eliminations of freedom.

The elimination of a freedom by a social agent may give rise to a variety of perceived intentions and these would presumably vary as a function of the conditions under which the elimination occurred. The important aspect of perceived intentions from the present point of view is that they may increase or decrease the implication that there will be threats or eliminations of additional freedoms. No attempt need be made here to spell out the conditions under which various kinds of intentions will be perceived, particularly since discussions of this may be found elsewhere (e.g., Heider, 1958), and an illustration should suffice to make the point. If Smith is told by his employer to stop smoking cigars in the office, Smith might imagine that this is because one of the secretaries is allergic to cigar smoke and that this elimination of his freedom therefore implies no eliminations or threats to other freedoms. On the other hand, Smith might imagine that his employer intends to stop his smoking altogether, i.e., cigarettes as well as cigars and out of the office as well as in. In the latter case Smith would experience a considerable degree of reactance since so many of his freedoms would be threatened. Clearly, then, it would be important to know how Smith perceived the intentions of his employer when the elimination occurred.

In conjunction with perceived intentions, personal eliminations of freedom may easily give rise to implied eliminations or threats to other freedoms because the instigator of the elimination is frequently one with whom a person expects future interaction. If, for example, Smith is told by his wife, "I don't like the smell of a cigar and I don't want you to smoke that cigar," there is the definite implication that neither can he smoke this cigar nor any other cigar in her presence in the future.

Social organizations, because they may be spread geographically and also because they may serve a variety of needs, can easily produce implied eliminations. If, for example, an insurance agent in Durham has decided he does not want to insure Smith's car against accident, it is quite clearly implied that Smith's freedom to have his car insured by the same company through agents in other locations is also eliminated, and it may also be implied that this same agent or others working for the same company would not insure Smith's boat, house, etc. The single actual elimination of one freedom implies the elimination of a variety of freedoms which could be served by the same organization.

Since a direct re-establishment of freedom is not possible when the freedom has been eliminated, the only obvious consequence of the reactance created is that the eliminated freedom will increase in attractiveness and the individual will tend to feel increasingly that he is master of his own fate. Of course, these subjective effects, which to one degree or another are discrepant with the realities of the situation, may be somewhat short-lived.

The re-establishment of a freedom can sometimes be attempted by indirect methods if the eliminated behavior belongs to a class of behaviors and the individual can manage to engage in one or more of the remaining behaviors within that class. Whether or not he can, of course, will depend upon his power relative to the agent which imposed the elimination, and upon surveillance by that agent. Consider, for example, the adolescent girl who has been told by her parents that she is still too young to date even though many of her peers do so (which implies to her that she has the freedom to date). This stricture implies that she is too young for hugging, kissing, petting, etc., with boys. But unless the parents constantly survey her non-dating activity with boys, she can attempt to regain her freedom by engaging in these more "advanced" activities.

When a behavioral freedom has been eliminated by someone of relatively low power, there will be the same tendency to re-establish one's freedom. However, this will not take the form of engaging in other behaviors of the same class, since one's relatively high power insures that one can do this anyway. Rather, it will take the form of attempting to avoid future eliminations of a similar kind. This means, in effect, that one will remind the person who performed the elimination that he is not allowed to do such things and that there are penalties for doing so. Punishment may be meted out and surveillance or other steps may be taken to insure that the necessary possibility for recurrence does not take place. Thus where a child has purposely failed to relay a telephone message to his mother, the latter may punish the child, and she may be careful to answer the telephone herself in the future.

Although many of the more interesting implications of our analysis have to do with attempts to re-establish freedom, these implications tend to be relatively complicated and might therefore serve as less satisfactory tests of the theory. As with impersonal elimination of freedom, however, it is possible to make a relatively simple test in terms of the subjective aspects of reactance. A search of the literature has failed to turn up evidence which would serve this purpose, although there are many studies which could be interpreted in terms of reactance theory. For example, many experiments on frustration involve a personal elimination of a behavioral freedom, and the consequent aggressive tendencies could be seen as an index of the motivation to re-establish this freedom. But no published studies have been found in which it is possible to separate the effects of elimination of freedom from those of frustration. This, of course, is not strange since the studies were designed to examine effects of frustration and not to rule out or detect effects of elimination of freedom.

However, we have designed and carried out two related experiments to test the effect of a personal elimination of freedom on the subsequent attractiveness of choice alternatives. Since these experiments were conducted in a two-alternative choice setting, let us first consider how reactance theory would apply when there are two alternatives.

Let us assume there are two choice alternatives which are attractive, and that they satisfy different needs, so that it should be of some importance to the individual that he be free to choose each. Now if only one of the two can be selected, then the other must necessarily be rejected. The two behaviors free to the individual, then, are to select A while rejecting B, or to select B while rejecting A. The importance of each freedom will then be a direct function of how attractive the alternatives are and how equal they are in attractiveness. For to the extent that it is difficult for the individual to decide which alternative he will take, it is important that he be free to select either and reject either.

The elimination of either alternative should arouse reactance, and the magnitude of the reactance will depend upon the importance of the freedom to select the eliminated alternative as well as the importance of the freedom to reject the alternative which remains and must now be taken. Given that A is more attractive than B, if B is eliminated, there will be less reactance aroused than if A is eliminated. Furthermore, where the alternatives are A and B, and B is eliminated, reactance should manifest itself in greater desire for B and a decrease in desire for A. This should be true whether A or B is the more attractive to begin with.

The following two experiments were carried out by Hammock and Brehm (1966). Both experiments obtained preference rankings of several items, promised the subject choice or no choice about which of two items he would receive as a gift, presented one of the two alternatives without choice, and then obtained re-rankings of the items. We shall describe them separately.

In the first experiment, the subjects were 12 boys and 15 girls ranging in age from 7 to 11, obtained from a supervised summer playground. The experimenter took the children one at a time to a building which was part of the recreational facility. The subject was seated at a table and, after a short warm-up conversation, the experimenter gave the following instructions to subjects in the Choice condition:

"I bet you like candy bars, don't you? I'm going to give you a candy bar if you'll do something for me. In fact, I'm going to let you choose between two different kinds of candy bars if you'll do something for me. In that room (pointing to a door) there are two different kinds of candy bars, and you can have whichever one you want if you'll do what I want you to. Here's what I want you to do for me: I'm trying to find out what kinds of candy bars young people your age like best. I've got a bunch of different candy bars in this bag, and if you'll tell me which ones you like best, I'll let you choose one of the two candy bars in the other room. If I let you choose one of the two candy bars in the other room, will you tell me which candy bars in this bag you like best when I show them to you?" The subject always agreed to this proposition.

In the No Choice condition, the instructions were the same except that subjects were told they would be given one of the two kinds of candy bars rather than that they would be able to choose.

Nine popular candy bars were then laid out in a row on the table in front of the subject, and he was asked to point to the one he liked best. This one was removed, and the subject was then asked to point to which of the remaining bars he liked best. This procedure was repeated until all nine bars had been ranked in preference.

At this point, ostensibly to get a form, the experimenter went into the room where the candy was and informed a female assistant which bars had been ranked third and fourth most attractive. When the experimenter returned with the form, he informed the subject that a girl in the other room would show him the two candy bars and depending upon the condition, would let him choose or would give him one. The experimenter then turned the subject over to the assistant with the instruction either that the subject was to choose whichever of two bars he wanted, or that he was to be given his candy bar. The experimenter stayed in the first room and the door between the rooms was closed.

The assistant then showed the subject that the bars she had were those which he had ranked third and fourth. She said: "Now we have two different kinds of candy. We have————and————. Now let me see... I think I'm going to give you the————." She always named the rank 3 bar, the preferred one. She then put the bar in a paper bag, took the subject out to the first room, and returned to her own room, again closing the door behind her.

The experimenter then explained to the subject that he had made a mistake in recording the preferences and would like the subject to give his preferences again. The same ranking procedure was used. If the subject asked if he should try to remember what he had done the first time, he was told to give his preferences according to his present feelings.

In summary, all subjects in the experiment were told that the two kinds of candy available as a gift were the bars which they had initially ranked numbers 3 and 4 out of nine. Futhermore, all subjects were given the rank 3 bar, the one which they presumably preferred. In giving it to them, however, the assistant very obviously made the decision herself without reference to the subject's desires. From the subject's point of view, her decision was completely arbitrary. But it should be emphasized that this was true for both conditions. The only difference between conditions was that subjects were led to believe either that they would be given one of the two kinds of bars available, or that they would be able to choose between the two kinds available.

In the No Choice condition it would be plausible for the attractiveness of the gift bar (rank 3) to increase because of ownership or anticipation of eating it, etc., and for the attractiveness of the eliminated bar (rank 4) to decrease because of disappointment at not getting it, decrease in anticipation of eating it, etc. However, we had no particular expectations about changes in rankings in the No Choice condition: its purpose was to serve as a low reactance baseline. For in the Choice condition, subjects should have experienced reactance and a consequent tendency to evaluate the eliminated bar (rank 4) higher and the bar forced on them (rank 3) lower. These expected shifts of evaluation in the Choice condition could then be expected to appear as differences from the comparable changes in the No Choice condition.

The mean rank changes of the gift and eliminated bars are shown in Table IX. The data for the No Choice condition show that there is a

TABLE IX

MEAN ATTRACTION CHANGES OF THE ELIMINATED AND
GIFT CANDY BARS

|  | Eliminated (rank 4) | Gift (rank 3) | Total reactance effect |
|---|---|---|---|
| No Choice (N = 14) | − .43 | .00 | − .43 |
| Choice (N = 13) | .23 | − 1.23 | 1.46 |

tendency for evaluation of the eliminated bar to decrease, although there is no tendency for the gift bar to change either way. In the Choice condition, however, the results are quite different: the eliminated bar shows increased evaluation while the gift bar shows decreased evaluation. The Total Reactance Effect is any increase in evaluation of the eliminated bar plus any decrease in evaluation of the gift bar, and these data, shown in the third column of Table IX, indicate that Choice subjects experienced more reactance than No Choice subjects ($t = 2.27$, $df = 25$ $p < .05$). The Total Reactance Effect for the Choice condition, 1.46, means that on the average, subjects in this condition tended to interchange the ranks of the eliminated and gift bars, since a simple interchange of the rank 3 and 4 bars by all subjects in the condition would result in a score of 2.00.

The results are clearly as predicted. But is it possible that they are due to something other than reactance? Disappointment or frustration are not likely responsible since subjects in both conditions received the initially preferred bar of the two offered. Sheer differential involvement as a function of having choice or not would not account for the results since the trend effects in the No Choice condition are not in the same direction as those in the Choice condition. It is quite possible, of course, that subjects in the Choice condition felt some hostility toward the assistant for usurping their choice. But the second rankings, like the first, were taken by the experimenter while the assistant remained in the other room behind a closed door. Nor, from the subject's point of view, did the experimenter know that his choice had been usurped or even which bar he had been given. In any case, it is not clear why hostility per se would produce any change in evaluation of the alternatives. While a single experimental test cannot stand as sufficient evidence for a theoretical proposition, it would seem that the present experiment does lend support to the hypothesis that personal elimination of freedom arouses reactance and consequent re-evaluation of objects of the relevant behaviors.

The second experiment started out to be a simple replication of the first, but with another subject population. Where the first was carried out with children from relatively low income families, the second was carried out with children from relatively high income families. The subjects, ranging in age from 8 to 12, and all male, were obtained at a boys' club and the experiment was run at the club.

An initial attempt to replicate produced no difference between conditions. With a little interviewing of the subjects, it became apparent that candy bars were not appropriate choice alternatives since it was not unusual for these subjects to eat as many as two or three candy bars a day. Toys, costing about $1 each, were then tried as alternatives. Again, however, no clear difference was obtained. While occasional subjects in the Choice condition evidenced some reactance, by and large, subjects still did not seem to be affected by the usurpation of choice. We found ourselves in the dilemma of not being able to offer alternatives which were attractive (and the loss of which would make a difference to our subjects) but still reasonable and plausible as a gift for a brief and simple task (ranking the items).

As we have said, theoretically, the importance of the freedom to have an item is a function not only of the absolute attractiveness of the item but also of its relative attractiveness compared to the other selections possible. When the less attractive of two alternatives is eliminated, the effect of importance from relative attractiveness is minimized. However, if the more attractive of two alternatives were eliminated, this source of importance would be maximized. It was therefore decided to eliminate the rank 3 item instead of the rank 4.

The experimental procedure was similar to that of the first study. Ten toys were shown to the subject, and he was told that he would be given one for ranking them according to his preferences. However, as an additional control on subjects' expectations, they were told that the toys to be given as gifts were two of the ten to be rated but might not be the ones they liked most. Some were told they would be able to choose between two while others were told they would simply be given one. After the initial ranking, and after the experimenter surreptitiously told the assistant which toys had been ranked third and fourth, the subject was sent into a second room with the assistant to choose or be given a toy. The third- and fourth-ranked toys were displayed and the assistant said, "Here are the toys. Hmmm. Well, they both look the same to me. I guess I'm going to give you this one." She gave the subject his fourth-ranked toy, the less preferred one. As in the first experiment, the subject was then returned to the first room where he was asked by the experimenter to rank the toys again because of an error in recording his preferences the first time. Also as before, the assistant remained in her own room with the door closed.

Although the more preferred alternative was eliminated, our expectations may be stated as before. No particular changes in evaluation were expected in the No Choice condition, although it would be plausible to find that the eliminated toy decreased and the gift toy increased. In the Choice condition, it would be expected that the eliminated toy would increase in value while the gift toy would decrease, compared to the changes in the No Choice condition.

The mean rank changes, presented in Table X, yield support for these expectations. In the No Choice condition there is a tendency for the eliminated toy to decrease in value while the gift toy shows no change. This pattern is quite similar to that for the first experiment. In the Choice condition, there is only a slight lowering of the evaluation of the eliminated toy and a clear lowering for the gift toy. Although the eliminated toy fails to show positive change, as it did in the first experiment, its negative change is less in the Choice condition than in the No Choice condition. Indeed, as may be seen in the Total Reactance Effect index (change in gift toy subtracted from change in eliminated toy), the difference between conditions ($t = 2.73$, $df = 43$, $p < .01$) is quite like that of the first experiment, and is completely consistent with our theoretical expectations.

TABLE X

MEAN ATTRACTION CHANGES OF THE ELIMINATED AND GIFT TOYS

|  | Eliminated (rank 3) | Gift (rank 4) | Total reactance effect |
|---|---|---|---|
| No Choice ($N = 17$)[a] | −.94 | .00 | −.94 |
| Choice ($N = 28$) | −.11 | −.86 | .75 |

[a] The discrepancy in $N$'s between conditions is a random fluctuation. The experimenter flipped a coin to determine the condition for each subject.

It will undoubtedly have been noticed that subjects in this replication were frustrated by the elimination of their preferred alternative. This frustration, however, should not be different between conditions since subjects in both conditions were shown their third- and fourth-ranked toys as those being given away, prior to their being given the fourth ranked. On the other hand, if we compare the results of the second experiment with those of the first, in which frustration was not involved, we might argue that elimination of a preferred alternative tends to result in a greater tendency for devaluation than does elimination of a non-preferred alternative. That is, frustration may produce devaluation of the goal-object. But this interpretation is necessarily speculative since the absolute attractiveness of alternatives in the two experiments is not held constant.

In the interests of experimental simplicity, the present eliminations of freedom were not of a strongly personal nature. There was no attempt, for example, to establish or manipulate any particular kind of interaction or power relationship between the subject and the assistant who usurped his choice. Of course, it was clear that the assistant had the power to eliminate the child's freedom, but at the same time, it probably appeared to the child that the experimenter was more powerful than the assistant. This was one reason for keeping the experimenter and assistant in separate rooms with a closed door between. For if the assistant has usurped the child's choice in front of the experimenter, the child would surely have expected the experimenter to intervene on his behalf. But as noted earlier, from the child's point of view, the experimenter did not know the assistant had usurped his choice. The child presumably thought that he had been victimized by an assistant who disobeyed the experimenter's instructions to allow choice. What the child may have thought about the assistant for her arbitrary usurpation of choice we do not know. It is conceivable that in the first experiment the child's changes in preference resulted from perceiving the assistant's decision as reflecting her own preferences and from the child's wanting to be different from the assistant. But in the second experiment we attempted to control perception of the assistant's preference by having her explicitly say she couldn't see any difference between the alternative toys. Since the results of the two experiments are quite similar, it would seem that this factor of perceived preference on the part of the assistant was not very important and probably does not account for the results of the first experiment.

That subjects in the Choice conditions may have thought the behavior of the assistant a little strange cannot be denied, and it therefore remains possible that there was some complicating factor of which we are unaware that could account for our results. But, as we have noted, every attempt was made to keep the experimental procedure as simple as possible while at the same time creating a personal elimination of freedom. Since we have not found a plausible alternative explanation, we tentatively conclude that these two experiments support the proposition that a personal elimination of a behavioral freedom arouses reactance.

## Summary

Our theoretical analysis of personal elimination of freedom pointed out that while direct re-establishment of freedom is impossible, indirect re-establishment will sometimes be possible, and whether or not indirect methods are attempted will depend upon the power of the person or organization which produced the elimination, and upon the ability of that person or organization to survey the activities of the individual whose freedom is reduced. Also, since personal eliminations are likely to occur in the context of stable social relationships, it will frequently be true that a personal elimination will imply elimination of future behavioral freedoms as well. This, of course, will increase the magnitude of reactance. When the person who performs the elimination has relatively low power, we may expect the one whose freedom is eliminated to avoid future repetitions of the elimination by dramatizing his power over the other, by increasing his surveillance over the other, and by decreasing the other's access to control over things and events related to important behavioral freedoms. Whether re-establishment of freedoms is possible or not, the subjective effects of reactance should occur and be detectable. Since concentration on the subjective effects also simplifies an experimental test, we chose to examine the effects of personal elimination of freedom on the attractiveness of choice alternatives in our first research.

Two experiments were described in which subjects were led to believe they would be able to choose between two attractive items, or that they would simply be given one of the two attractive items, and in which one of the two items was then personally eliminated.

In both experiments the value of the eliminated item became relatively more attractive when subjects expected choice than when they did not expect choice. The value of the gift item decreased more for those who expected choice than for those who did not. Since both effects were predicted, and plausible alternative explanations were not found, these results were interpreted as support for reactance theory.

# CHAPTER IV

# Personal Threat to Freedom

In the previous two chapters we discussed irrevocable eliminations of freedoms and indicated some differences between those which are personal and those which are impersonal. We now take up the notion of *threats* of elimination of freedom and, in particular, those threats which may be seen as personal.

A threat to a behavioral freedom is characterized by the fact that eventual elimination of the freedom need not occur. This will be true whether the threat consists of an impending elimination of freedom which can be avoided or an elimination of freedom which has already occurred but which is revokable. With a threat, then, there is the possibility of direct re-establishment of freedom—i.e., the individual can engage in the behavior which has been threatened with exclusion. In this chapter we shall give particular consideration to personal threats to one's freedom: how they may occur, how they affect the magnitude of reactance, and what the effects of such reactance may be.

The concept of a personal threat to freedom implies a formal or informal power relationship between the threatener and the person threatened. That is, the threat is meaningful only to the extent that (1) the threatener has some possibility of carrying it out and/or making it hold, and (2) the threatener is likely to carry out the threat. The absence of either of these conditions would make any attempted threat meaningless. Thus, the threatener must have some degree of control over the behavior which he is threatening to eliminate, or he must have control over other benefits or penalties such that he can gain some degree of control over the behavior to be eliminated. An employer, for example, may have direct control over the length of

51

coffee breaks of an employee, and be able to attempt to shorten them at will. Since he could have the employee punch a time clock for coffee breaks, he has relatively direct control over this behavior. The employer might also attempt to keep his employees from participating in public activities such as civil rights demonstrations. In this case, however, he has no direct control and must depend upon his power to control other benefits, such as salary and promotion, or penalties, such as firing, to back up his attempted restriction of behavior. Here too, no doubt, the employee would feel there was a real threat to his freedom. However, our present purpose is not to carry out a detailed analysis of social power, which has been done by others (e.g., Thibaut and Kelley, 1959), but simply to point out that threats to eliminate free behaviors depend upon social power.

Given that another person has some degree of control over one's behavioral possibilities, it is still necessary that he be perceived as likely to use that control in order for any attempted threat to have meaning. A "threat" from a person who has formal power to carry it out but who, for one reason or another, is unlikely to carry it out, will not be taken seriously. The office supervisor who wants to be liked by his workers, for example, may be unable to pose a serious threat to their freedom to take long coffee breaks.

It might be thought that the perceived intention of a threat to eliminate a free behavior would be important in determining the magnitude of consequent reactance, and in a sense it is. For, as noted in the preceding chapter, the perceived intent may have implications for threats to further free behaviors, either minimizing or suggesting further threats. But complete minimization of further threats does not eliminate the present one, and the individual should experience reactance from the present threat no matter how benign the threatener's intentions are perceived to be.

Reactance produced by a threat can result in direct re-establishment of freedom, that is, generally, by engaging in the free behavior threatened with elimination. Whether or not direct re-establishment of freedom will be attempted will depend upon the following factors:

1. The likelihood that the attempt will be successful. This is a rephrasing of the fact that there is a threat rather than an irrevocable elimination of freedom. From the point of view of the person experiencing reactance, there will be greater and lesser probabilities that he could actually engage in the threatened free behavior. To take an

example, when a child has been told by his parent not to play outside the yard, the child may be uncertain as to whether or not he will be physically restrained from doing so. To the extent that he thinks it possible, he will be more inclined to try playing outside the yard in order to restore any freedom he has felt threatened.

2. The estimated cost to oneself of engaging in the threatened behavior. In addition to the normal effort of engaging in the behavior, there may be implicit or explicit threats of loss of rewards or of punishments for not giving up the threatened freedom. Thus the child in the above example may refrain from straying from the yard because he fears consequent punishment. It should be clear, however, that with the amount of this fear held constant, the greater is the magnitude of reactance, the more likely he is to leave the yard.

3. The ease and likelihood of regaining freedom in other ways. When other ways of re-establishing one's freedom are available, and when these ways are relatively easy and likely to serve successfully in the re-establishment of freedom, attempts at direct restoration will be less likely. Consider again the child of the above example. If he is quite certain of being punished for leaving the yard, then instead of doing so he may search for a safer way of re-establishing his freedom. Perhaps, for example, he could engage in a more forbidden behavior (which will help re-establish his freedom by implication), such as eating worms, without much fear of detection.

4. Attempts to restore freedom directly or by implication may not occur, even when they are possible, because the restraint from expected costs of engaging in the behavior is greater then the magnitude of reactance. Under these conditions, of course, the subjective effects of reactance would still be expected to occur.

In summary, attempts at direct restoration of a behavioral freedom will tend to occur when the probability of success is high and the expected cost low relative to other ways in which freedom might be regained, and when the magnitude of reactance is great enough to overcome restraint from the cost.

Before we leave the general discussion of the effects of social threats to freedom, it may be well to consider the implications for the general social influence paradigm. Since the problem of persuasive communications and attitude change will be covered in Chapter VI, the present discussion will center on attempts to obtain behavioral compliance without prior attitude change.

Whenever a person is subjected to attempts on the part of another to make him behave in a particular way, he may perceive the attempts as a threat to his freedom, and he should then experience reactance and show some consequent attempt to re-establish that freedom. Thus, if the magnitude of reactance is relatively great, the individual can be expected to show little or no compliance and he may even show anti-compliant behavior. If the magnitude of reactance is relatively low, there will simply be some reduction in the amount of compliance shown.

It will be recognized that, according to this analysis, reactance should occur quite frequently in social influence situations and its effects should be visible in at least some of the rather large number of social influence experiments in the literature. While such effects may indeed be visible in terms of "reduced" and even "negative" social influence, the interpretation of these effects in terms of reactance is generally confounded by the possibility of a variety of other processes which may also account for them. Since no published studies have been found in which the attempt to influence was intended differentially to reduce freedom, there is almost inevitably some ambiguity about interpreting the attempted influence in terms of reactance. Nor have any examples been found which could be clearly interpreted as manipulating the amount or importance of the freedom which was threatened by the influence attempt. Such studies, if available, might furnish relatively cogent tests of the theory.

We turn, therefore, to some experiments explicitly designed to test the effects of social threats to behavioral freedoms. In keeping with the introductory discussion, these tests are primarily concerned with measures of direct re-establishment of freedom.

### Attempted Usurpation of Choice

If a person is free to choose between two alternatives, A and B, an attempt by another person to tell him which to choose constitutes a threat to this freedom. At the same time, if there is no apparent selfish reason why the second person would want the first to pick a particular alternative, the influence attempt may be taken by the first to indicate that there is some reason for compliance, that is, there is informational value and possibly one or more motivational elements in the influence attempt in support of compliance. The informational and motivational aspects may occur concurrently with the perception that there is an influence attempt, with the consequence that the positive effect of the influence attempt and the counter effect of reactance may tend to cancel each other out in determining resultant compliance. The result is that if a direct attempt to influence a person's choice is to yield clear reactance effects, it must minimize positive influence effects from the informational aspect, or control for them.

A more cogent test of the effect of a social influence attempt on the magnitude of reactance can be constructed by manipulating the importance of the freedom to make the choice. With the influence attempt held constant, the greater is the importance of the freedom to choose, the greater should be the magnitude of reactance and consequent attempt to re-establish the freedom.

The direct re-establishment of freedom with a two-alternative choice, A and B, is specific: if the individual is told to choose A, almost the only way he can re-establish his freedom is by choosing B. The slight exception is that he may try to convince himself that he can ignore the influence attempt and choose independently. However, it will be difficult for a person to convince himself that he has not been positively influenced if he chooses the alternative he was told to choose.

The testable hypothesis, then, is that when a person is free to choose either A or B, if he is told to choose A, he will experience reactance and will, consequently, tend to choose B. This tendency to select the alternative opposite to that suggested will increase as the importance of the freedom to choose increases. Accordingly, the following experiment was conducted by Barbara Burton.[4]

Female introductory psychology students were recruited to participate in a reseach project. When a subject arrived for her experimental session, she found another girl sitting, studying, in one of the chairs outside the experimental room. The waiting girl, a confederate of the experimenter, was a freshman with a relatively naive appearance. Immediately after the subject arrived, the experimenter put her head out of the door and asked the two subjects to enter the experimental room. They were placed at separate tables. In the Low Importance condition, the experimenter said she was collecting information preparatory to a later experiment, and that each was simply to inspect two tasks, choose one of them and perform it. In the High Importance conditions, she said they were about to take The

[4]Burton, Barbara L. "Reactance to attempted reduction of degree of choice." Unpublished Undergraduate Honors Thesis, Duke University, 1962.

Stanford Projective Personality Test, and that it had been determined that which task a person chose and how he performed on it were indicative of certain important aspects of personality. They were also told to write their name on the test if they wanted the results.

The two Tasks, entitled "A" and "B," consisted of a page of the same typed material and required the crossing out of certain letters. They differed only in that Task A consisted of marking out the letters *c* and *n*, Task B, letters *d* and *p*. Pretesting had indicated there would be no preference between these two tasks.

The experimenter handed the test materials to the confederate, then finished the instructions and said she was going to leave while they worked, and, finally, handed the test materials to the subject. While the instructions were being finished, the confederate glanced through her test materials, and, immediately after the experimenter left and closed the door behind her, the confederate said, "I think we should do Task A (or B). Oh dear! I see we're not supposed to talk. Oh, well, I guess it doesn't matter." The confederate then proceeded to work. This attempted influence by the confederate constituted the pressure to choose a given alternative and was carried out with part of the subjects in each the Low and High Importance conditions. The task dictated by the confederate was alternated within each condition of importance. For control subjects, the confederate said nothing but simply proceeded to work.

The interesting question is which task is chosen by the subject after she hears the influence attempt by the confederate—the one suggested by the confederate or the opposite one? If the influence attempt does arouse reactance, then the subject should tend to select the opposite alternative.

In the control conditions, 11 subjects chose Task A and 9 chose Task B, indicating that there was no preference for one or the other, nor was there any difference as a function of importance. The results for the influence conditions may be seen in Table XI. They show that subjects exposed to the influence attempt tended to do the *opposite* of what was suggested (for all experimental subjects, $\chi^2 = 3.70, p = .06$). Furthermore, this effect is weak in the Low Importance condition ($p > .25$), and fairly clear in the High Importance condition ($p = .06$), lending support to the expectation that the magnitude of reactance is a direct function of the importance of having choice.

Though the evidence is consistent with the prediction, various questions may be raised about the interpretation and generality of the

TABLE XI

NUMBER OF SUBJECTS CHOOSING SUGGESTED OR OPPOSITE TASK

|  | Task chosen | |
|---|---|---|
|  | Suggested | Opposite |
| Low importance | 5 | 8 |
| High importance | 3 | 11 |
| Combined | 8 | 19 |

effects. One problem is that only one confederate was used and the effects may therefore be due to the particular characteristics of this person. However, the tendency for the effect to be greater in the High than in the Low Importance condition, although not reliable statistically, argues in favor of the reactance interpretation. But this argument is weakened by the fact that the confederate was aware of which condition was being run and may conceivably have acted differently in the two conditions. There is the additional possibility that the subject thought the confederate a witless blabbermouth, and this gave the subject some reason for choosing differently where the choice indicated something about personalities, but not where the choice did not have this significance. There is nothing in the present data to rule out such an alternative explanation, although every attempt was made to have the confederate behave like a normal, pleasant person except for the attempted usurpation of choice.

In order to obtain further confirmation of the effects of attempted usurpation of choice, and in order to try to eliminate some of the ambiguity of interpretation of the above experiment, the following study was designed and conducted by Brehm and Sensenig (1967). The basic design of the previous experiment for usurping choice was utilized, but several steps were taken to make this experiment a more cogent test of reactance theory: (1) the subject was never allowed to see the other (fictitious) subject who attempted the usurpation of choice; (2) the subject's impression of the fictitious subject was controlled by giving him what was supposed to be an autobiographical sketch by the fictitious subject; (3) the communication from the fictitious subject was written and therefore invariant; (4) the positive influence value of the attempted influence was held more nearly equal between reactance and control conditions, and in addition a measure of positive social influence was obtained; and, finally, (5) the manipulation of importance of freedom, which was somewhat ambiguous, was dropped in favor of a manipulation of implied loss of freedom, which promised less ambiguity of interpretation.

According to our analysis in Chapter I, the greater is the number of free behaviors lost by implication, the greater will be the magnitude of reactance. Therefore, to manipulate the amount of freedom lost by implication in the present setting, all subjects were led to expect they would make five decisions, but some were told they would receive a communication from another person only for the first decision (low implication) while others were told they would receive a communication for each of the five decisions (high implication). Given that the communication is designed to threaten the subject's freedom on the first decision, if he knows that he will receive no communications for the remaining four decisions, then these future freedoms are not threatened. But if he knows he is to receive a communication on each future decision, then he may well imagine that these future freedoms are also threatened when the communication for the first decision attempts to usurp his first choice. The procedure for the whole experiment was as follows.

High school students were recruited to take part in a "psychological research project." When the subject arrived he was ushered into one room in a suite of research rooms. The experimenter explained that he was interested in how people form impressions of each other and that he would ask the subject to look at some pictures and make certain decisions about what the people in these pictures might be thinking, feeling, or doing. The subject was then shown two sample pictures and asked to decide with which picture he could do the better job of guessing what the people were thinking, feeling, and doing. When he had selected one of the two pictures, he was given three brief alternative descriptions of what might be going on in that picture, and was asked to choose the one which fit best. The experimenter then explained that this was the procedure which would be followed, and that there were five pairs of pictures to choose between and make judgements about. In order to increase the importance of the choices he also indicated that he was quite interested in which pictures would be chosen because "we can tell quite a bit about a person by which pictures he chooses . . . and how well a person does on matching the stories to the picture depends on a person choosing a picture he understands."

It was necessary to give the subject a plausible reason for his receiving a communication from another person which would be relevant to the choices between the paired pictures. This communication would contain the attempt to influence the subject's choice. However, the influence attempt itself could not be made a part of the experiment from the subject's point of view because that would mean that he was not free to make his choice independently. Neither did we want the other person to appear as an expert in regard to the influence attempt since the resultant positive influence effect would tend to hide any reactance effect. These requirements were satisfied in the following way.

After the subject understood the experimental task the experimenter said he was also interested in finding out how well a person could guess which pictures another person could do well on if he knew something about that other person. The subject was then told that another student of the same sex and grade from his school had come in 15 or 20 minutes earlier and was in a room down the hall. It was made clear that neither would ever learn the name of the other. The experimenter explained that the other person had been asked to write a short description of himself which would then be given to the subject, and based upon this information, the subject would decide which picture of each pair that person would do best on, and that person would then be asked to judge the pictures selected. It was impressed on the subject that he might either choose the same picture or the opposite picture for himself and the other person. The experimenter then left the room and returned with the (fictitious) self-description, which he left with the subject for study. The self-description portrayed a typical teenager.

After about five minutes the experimenter returned to the room with the set of pictures. The subject was given a form on which to indicate which of each pair he selected for himself, and which for the other person. The experimenter then said that since many people felt a need for more information in order to select the right picture for the other person, he had just now shown the pictures to the other person and allowed him to write a note to express his preference on each pair. However, it was explained, the subject was to make the final judgment for the other person and need not follow the other person's suggestion. The procedure then consisted of the subject's reading the note from the other person, looking at the pair of pictures and selecting one for himself and one for the other, and then repeating this operation for the next set, etc., until the five sets were completed. Actually, the pairs of pictures were matched so there would be little or no preference for either.

Three conditions were arranged. In the Control, the first note said "I prefer 1-A (or 1-B)." In the High Implication condition, the first note said "I think we should both do 1-A (or 1-B)." Subjects in the Control and High Implication conditions expected, and received, a note for each of the five pairs of pictures. The notes for pairs 2 through 5 stated simple preferences, such as "I would prefer 2-A," and the stated preferences between A and B were randomly arranged for each subject. In the Low Implication condition, subjects were told that the other person had been shown only the first pair of pictures and that they would receive a note for only that pair. This note was identical to the first note for the High Implication conditions.

Before looking at the results of this study, let us summarize our theoretical expectations. Subjects in the Control condition were exposed to a simple statement of preference by the "other." Thus, this condition allows us to assess the extent to which the other's preference tended to produce positive social influence, and gives us a baseline against which to compare the counterinfluence effects of reactance. In the Low Implication condition, subjects were exposed to the same preference expressed by the "other," but in addition, they were exposed to an attempted usurpation of their own choice, an attempt to get them to select for themselves the same picture preferred by the "other." This attempted usurpation, according to our theoretical analysis, should arouse reactance and a consequent tendency on the part of the subject to choose the opposite picture to that suggested. In the High Implication condition, subjects expected to read a note before making each decision about a pair of pictures. Thus, when they read the first note, which attempted to usurp their choice as in the Low Implication condition, there was the possible implication that each further note would also attempt to usurp their choice. Thus, these subjects should have experienced more reactance from the first note than those in the Low Implication condition, and their tendency on the first choice to select the opposite picture to the one suggested should have been greater.

The choices of subjects for themselves on the first pair of pictures

TABLE XII

TYPE OF CHOICE FOR SELF ON THE FIRST PAIR OF PICTURES

|  | Compliance | Non-compliance |
| --- | --- | --- |
| Control | 22 | 8 |
| Low implication | 14 | 16 |
| High implication | 12 | 18 |

is shown in Table XII. Subjects in the Control condition show a fairly strong positive social influence effect, as is reasonable, with more than two thirds of them selecting the same picture for themselves as is preferred by the other person. The reactance conditions, on the other hand, yield quite different effects. Both show a strong shift toward the non-compliant selection, the Low Implication condition being different from the Control at the 7% level ($\chi^2 = 3.40$), and the High Implication condition differing from the Control at the 2% level ($\chi^2 = 6.09$). This pattern is precisely as expected. However, the difference between the High and Low Implication conditions is not statistically reliable.

Analysis of the results by sex of subject showed that the general difference between the Control and the two reactance conditions was about the same, but the difference between the Low and High Implication conditions is accounted for solely by the females, the males having shown a slight difference in the opposite direction. One reason why the experiment might have worked better with females than males is that females would plausibly have been more interested in the interpersonal judgment task and may have paid more attention to what the note said. Or it may simply be that females are more sensitive to reductions of freedom. In any case, the overall results fail to confirm the proposition that the magnitude of reactance is a direct function of the possibility of implied further usurpations of choice. But they do indicate that an attempted influence which usurps choice tends to produce rejection of the influence.

Before leaving this experiment, let us consider whether or not the present evidence is more strongly supportive of reactance theory than was the Burton experiment, described before. It will be recalled that the results of the Burton experiment could be explained as due to the subjects' desire to be different from the confederate. The desire to be different might plausibly have arisen because, in a sense, the confederate spoke out of turn and apparently rather thoughtlessly.

In the present experiment the (fictitious) other person committed a similar kind of social error in that he told the subject what to choose for both of them, an influence attempt which, as far as the subject knew, was inconsistent with the experimental instructions. The present experiment might have created the same desire to be different, then, as might have occurred in the Burton experiment. But in this case the desire to be different can be measured by the influence which the fictitious subject exerted by his notes regarding the last four pairs of pictures. These notes, it will be recalled, stated a simple preference for one picture or the other of each pair. If the subject wanted to be different from the other person because the other had committed this social error of attempted influence, then he would presumably tend to choose the opposite picture in those pairs after the first. A tabulation of subjects who disagreed with the other's preference on at least three of the four pairs fails to yield any support for this possibility: 13 of 30 Control subjects and only 9 of 30 High Implication subjects show this tendency. If we look only at the second pair of pictures where any tendency to be different should have been greatest, we find that 14 of the 30 Control subjects and 16 of the 30 High Implication subjects selected the opposite to that preferred by the other person. In short, there is no evidence here to indicate that subjects in the reactance conditions wanted to be different from the other person in regard to the choices.

Thus, while the evidence for the implication hypothesis is at best weak, the evidence for the hypothesis that attempted usurpation of choice creates reactance is relatively strong. Furthermore, since the present experiment failed to support the alternative view that people want to be different from the one who attempts to influence them, we may have increased confidence that the results of the Burton experiment also support the hypothesis regarding attempted usurpation of choice.

It is interesting to note that if the present experiment had depended upon subjects' showing a predominance of non-compliant choices in order to support the reactance hypothesis, then support would not have been forthcoming. The reactance conditions produced only a mild predominance of the non-compliant choice. However, the strong positive influence evidenced in the Control condition makes clear that reactance does have its expected effect, but that this effect is partially cancelled out by positive influence. In this respect, the present outcome is somewhat weaker than that of the Burton study in which the tendency to choose the opposite task of that suggested was significant at the 6% level.

## Required Choice of a Preferred Alternative

One characteristic of the Burton and of the Brehm and Sensenig experiments is that the choice alternatives were designed so that there would be little or no preference between them in the absence of the experimentally induced forces. But it should be clear from earlier discussions that reactance can be aroused in regard to the threat of elimination of a choice alternative when there are preferences. Indeed, if a person were told that he *had* to take what he actually preferred, he should experience reactance from the threat to his freedom not to take what he prefers, and from the threat to his freedom(s) to take other alternatives. Thus, we might expect that he would re-establish his freedom by taking something other than his preferred alternative. Although this derivation is interesting, the predicted effect, theoretically, should be relatively weak. For not only does the reactance have to overcome the individual's preference, but the amount of reactance which can be aroused in this way should be rather limited. This is because the freedoms which are threatened are not likely to be very important when the alternatives in question are attractive. There certainly is little importance to the freedom not to take what one prefers. Similarly, there will be relatively little importance to the freedoms to choose less preferred alternatives. With these cautions in mind, let us turn to an experiment by Weiner [5] which was explicitly designed to test the hypothesis that a social influence attempt to make a person choose what he prefers arouses reactance and a consequent tendency to choose something else.

The experimenter first announced to classes of first-grade students that she was working for some toy stores and wanted to find out what kinds of toys boys and girls liked. She told them that for helping her, each child would get to choose whichever toy he wanted for himself.

Each subject was then individually put through a procedure in which

[5] Weiner, Judith A. "Psychological reactance from involuntary restriction of choice alternatives" Unpublished Undergraduate Honors Thesis, Duke University, 1963.

he rank-ordered the toys in terms of how much he would like to have them. Different sets of seven toys were used for boys and for girls. After the ranking was completed, each subject was thanked and asked not to reveal his choices to other students. Approximately one week later, each subject was again asked to rank the toys, this second ranking also constituting the child's final choice of toys for himself. In the Control condition, the second session procedure was essentially identical to that of the first session. In the Reactance condition, after the subject was again shown the toys, but before he ranked them, the experimenter said: "Oh, by the way, you remember the day when all the boys (girls) came to look at the toys for the first time? Well, one of them said something to me about you. Let's see, he said, '(name of subject) *has* to choose the (name of the preferred toy). He can't *choose* anything else.' So I asked him why he said that, and he said he didn't know, just that '(name of S) has to choose it, that's all.'" These subjects were then put through the usual ranking procedure.

If, when a person believes he can choose whichever alternative he wants, being told he has to take the one he most prefers arouses reactance, then he should tend to choose a *less* preferred alternative in order to restore his freedom. We would therefore expect more of the subjects in the Reactance condition than in the Control to reduce their initially preferred toy to a lower ranking in the second session. Table XIII shows the number of subjects in each condition who reduced the ranking of the initially preferred toy and how much they reduced it.

A Mann-Whitney U test is significant at the 7% level, one tail, a *t*-test on the mean difference between conditions is significant at the 2% level, and a comparison of changers only (median split) is significant at the 5% level by a Chi square. Thus, though there were several in the Control condition who reduced their initially preferred toy by one rank, the

TABLE XIII

NUMBER OF SUBJECTS WHO REDUCED RANK OF CRITICAL TOY

| | Number of ranks critical toy is reduced | | | | | | |
|---|---|---|---|---|---|---|---|
| | 0 | −1 | −2 | −3 | −4 | −5 | −6 |
| Control ($N = 23$) | 15 | 6 | 2 | 0 | 0 | 0 | 0 |
| Reactance ($N = 24$) | 13 | 2 | 2 | 3 | 3 | 0 | 1 |

magnitude and number of rank-reductions in the Reactance condition appears to be greater, as predicted. Those subjects who were told they *had* to take what they most preferred, tended to reject it, that is, rank it lower.

These results, although admittedly weak, are consistent with the reactance hypothesis. At the same time, there are certain possible alternative interpretations. For example, subjects may have interpreted the attempted influence to mean that the other person preferred a different alternative which he did not want the subject to choose. Similarly, the subject may have thought the experimenter was trying to get rid of the suggested alternative, and that this implied there was something wrong with it. Unfortunately, there is nothing in the results to rule out any of these possibilities. However, we would argue that these kinds of alternative explanations have not been shown to account for results in other experiments which have been reported in this volume, and they are not particularly plausible here. All in all, then, the results of this experiment by Weiner may be taken as at least tentative support for the hypothesis that threatened elimination of the freedom not to take the choice alternative one prefers arouses reactance and a consequent tendency to reject the preferred alternative.

## The Threat of a Favor

Up to this point we have been discussing social threats to freedom which are relatively direct and unequivocal in their manifest intent to influence. These kinds of threats to free behaviors are convenient for testing hypotheses from the theory, but it should not be construed that obvious influence attempts are a precondition for threats to the elimination of behavioral freedoms. In many cases it will be true that the action of another person will threaten or eliminate one's freedom even though the other person may be perceived to have the best of intentions. The only requirement for the arousal of reactance is that one or more of a person's free behaviors be eliminated or threatened with elimination, regardless of the perceived reasons.

It is therefore possible for an individual to arouse reactance in another person by doing for him what would normally be called a favor. Whether or not receiving a favor from another arouses reactance in oneself depends simply on whether or not receiving the favor threatens to eliminate one or more of one's own free behaviors. It should be clear that the freedoms most likely to be affected by the reception of a favor are those regarding how one behaves toward the giver: in general, one's freedom to behave negatively toward the giver is threatened, as is one's freedom not to behave positively toward him. The direct re-establishment of freedom would then consist of acting unfavorably toward the giver, e.g., *avoiding* performance of a return favor.

It would be fair to say that the normal effect of a favor is to enhance one's impression of the person who performs it. Furthermore, to receive a favor tends to obligate one to return it. For both reasons, we might expect that when a favor does not arouse reactance, it will tend to increase the recipient's tendency to perform a return favor. Thus, when it is of relatively little importance to be free of obligation to another person, a favor from him will arouse little reactance but will create a tendency to return the favor. However, when it is of relatively great importance to be free of obligation to another person, a favor from him will arouse relatively high reactance and a consequent tendency to avoid doing a return favor, which will tend to counter the direct tendency to return the favor. This line of reasoning has been tested by the following experiment by Brehm and Cole (1966).

Male introductory psychology students were recruited to take part in "Research on Projective Testing." When a subject reported for his research session, he found a note on the door of the experimental room, asking him to wait outside the room, where chairs were provided. If the subject was late, he found another male student already waiting; if he was early, the other male student arrived after, read the note, and took a seat. This other student, who appeared to be a subject for the same experiment, was a confederate of the experimenter.

Immediately after the second person arrived, the experimenter put her head out of the door and after identifying the two people as subjects for her research, announced that there would be a short wait for the preparation of experimental materials. At this, the confederate asked if he might leave for a few minutes and the experimenter said he could as long as he wasn't gone long. The experimenter then sat down by the subject and engaged him in casual conversation. She reminded him that she was doing research on projective testing and said that in addition she had been asked by a friend to collect some information on first impression ratings, since she was running two strangers at a time. Then, to create greater or lesser degrees of importance for the subject to be free in regard to the confederate, she told some subjects (High Importance) that the first impression ratings were for Dr. Terrell, who had just received a large grant for his research, and that it was important that the subject do as careful and accurate a job of making the ratings as he could. Subjects in the Low Importance condition were told that the ratings were for a student-friend's sociology class research project, and were therefore of not much consequence. In both conditions the subject was told to base his impression ratings solely on the other person's answers to three questions each of them would be asked. The experimenter then excused herself and returned to the experimental room.

Within three or four minutes the confederate returned. In the No Favor conditions he simply took his chair without comment. In the Favor conditions he gave the subject a soft drink and he refused payment if any were offered. Immediately after the confederate returned, the experimenter invited the two into the experimental room, so there would be little opportunity for talking.

The experimenter reiterated that she was doing research on projective testing but that she was first asking them to make first impressions ratings of each other. The importance instructions were also briefly reiterated, and then each person was asked to answer orally where he would like to travel, what kind of woman he would like to marry, and what occupation he intended to choose. The confederate gave standard, innocuous answers to these questions. Each was then asked to fill out a set of rating forms which consisted of adjective check lists (friendly-unfriendly, mature-immature, etc.) and a set of questions intended to measure the extent to which the subject liked the confederate and wanted to associate with the confederate in a variety of settings, and checks on the Importance and Favor manipulations.

When the ratings were completed, the experimenter removed a shield between the subject and confederate, who were seated at opposite ends of a small table, and, placing a stack of typing paper in front of the confederate, said, while looking at him, "Will one of you stack these papers into ten piles of five for me please?" She then seated herself at some distance, apparently to do something else, but actually so that she could surreptitiously observe how many piles the confederate made up before the subject offered to help, if he did.

The confederate was then sent on an errand and the subject was informally interviewed to discover suspicion and general impressions of what had happened.

Theoretically, when the importance to be unobligated to the confederate is low, that is, when the first impression ratings are of little consequence, the favor should arouse little reactance but some obligation to return the favor. In other words, in the Low Importance condition, we would expect that subjects would show a greater tendency to help stack papers when they had received the favor than when they had not. But in the High Importance condition, where it should have been relatively important to the subject to be unobligated toward the confederate, the favor should arouse relatively high reactance and a consequent tendency to *avoid* helping to stack the papers.

In order to show that the favor can either increase or decrease the subjects' tendencies to help stack papers, it is necessary that there be some intermediate tendency to help the confederate in the absence of a favor. In pretesting it was found that the paper-stacking task would result in about half of the subjects offering to help, and so it was expected that in the No Favor conditions of the actual experiment, about half would help and there would be no difference as a function of Importance. The upper half of Table XIV shows that these expectations were confirmed: approximately half of the subjects in each of the two No Favor conditions helped to stack papers, and there is no difference as a function of Importance.

Also as expected, the effect of the Favor in the Low Importance condition is to increase the tendency to help the confederate stack

TABLE XIV

NUMBER OF PERSONS WHO PERFORMED THE FAVOR

|  | Low importance | High importance |
|---|---|---|
| No favor |  |  |
| Helped | 9 | 7 |
| Did not help | 6 | 8 |
| Favor |  |  |
| Helped | 14 | 2 |
| Did not help | 1 | 13 |

papers, that is, to create a tendency to perform a return favor. But in the High Importance condition, the effect of the favor is quite the opposite: it is clearly to decrease the tendency to help the confederate stack papers. In short, these results give rather strong support to our reactance theory analysis of the effect of a favor.

It is of interest to note what happened in regard to the first impression ratings. It had been expected that subjects might feel somewhat annoyed by the confederate when he aroused reactance in them, even though the situation was constructed such that the soft drink could only be seen as a friendly gesture, and that he might therefore tend to rate the confederate down on various dimensions. However, only one rating dimension, that of "friendly-unfriendly," supported this expectation. Whereas the favor increased the perceived friendliness in the Low Importance condition, it did not in the High Importance condition, the interaction being significant by analysis of variance at the 5% level. By and large, though, the impression ratings were simply unaffected by the amount of reactance aroused. The reason may simply be that the High Importance instructions stressed the need for accuracy, and the subjects complied by managing to ignore their reactance in making the impression ratings. But since the paper-stacking task did not appear to be part of the impression formation task, it allowed subjects to respond according to their motivational state.

The characterization of the threat in this experiment as personal may seem odd and in need of explanation. Actually, in designing the experiment there was no thought about making the threat explicitly personal or impersonal. The intent of the design was to see whether or not a favor from one person to another could arouse reactance. At the same time we wanted to avoid a complicated social relationship between the person giving the favor and the recipient in order to minimize the possibility that irrelevant factors would creep into the design and might then account for the results. The social relationship was therefore reduced to the bare minimum necessary for one person to present a favor to another. The favor might well be characterized as an impersonal threat except for the fact that the subject could still imagine that it was intended to obligate him toward the other. The fact that the confederate was apparently unaware of the impression formation task when he produced the favor only rules out an obvious motive; it does not rule out other motives which the subject could imagine. Similar observations could be made about some of the other experiments reported in this chapter: the threat to freedom was made relatively impersonal for the sake of simplicity in experimental design, but the threat could be perceived by the subject as personal.

## Summary

In this chapter we have tried to show how threats differ in their implications from actual elimination of free behaviors. Inherent in the notion of threat is the possibility that elimination can be avoided or revoked, and thus there is the possibility that reactance will lead to attempts at direct re-establishment of freedom, i.e., engaging in the threatened behavior. However, since a threat may or may not be carried through, its capability for arousing reactance is a direct function of the possibility that it can be carried through and the likelihood that it will be. The magnitude of a personal threat, then, will in part be a function of social power.

While a survey of the published literature on social influence has yielded little or nothing which can serve as a test of reactance theory, four experiments were described here which were explicitly designed to test the effects of personal threats to freedom. In each case it was found that there was a tendency for people to do the opposite of what was called for by the manifest pressure put on them. Additionally, in one study the importance of the relevant freedom had a weak but theoretically consistent effect, while in a second, importance had a clear, theoretically expected, effect. An attempt in another study to show that the magnitude of reactance is directly proportional to the amount of freedom threatened by implication yielded only suggestive results.

# CHAPTER V

# Impersonal Threat to Freedom

It will frequently happen that one or more of an individual's free behaviors is threatened with elimination by events which have nothing to do with him personally. This is obvious, of course, and is simply an extension of the proposition of Chapter II concerning impersonal elimination of freedom. However, the extension may not be obvious in all of its ramifications and we will therefore discuss certain aspects in some detail.

Impersonal threats, like personal threats, occur when an event which would eliminate a behavioral freedom is likely to occur in the future, or when an event which implies the elimination of behavioral freedom will definitely occur or has already occurred. In the latter case, the occurrence of the event creates a pressure on the individual to give up the behavioral freedom. For example, if a state law were passed that all automobile passengers had to wear seat belts whenever their vehicle were in motion, this does not actually put a seat belt around every car passenger but it does create a pressure for every passenger to have a seat belt around him. When the event for which there is pressure constitutes an elimination of freedom, then the pressure may be considered a threat to freedom.

Let us first consider those threats which are impersonal simply because they are the result of inanimate nature. The first question which must be raised about natural events is what freedom does one have in regard to them? Picture a person, for example, who is planning a picnic for the coming Sunday. His freedom to have a picnic is surely determined in part by the weather: if he lives in Minnesota and it is midwinter, he is not really free to have a picnic because the temperature

71

is quite sure to be low, and there may be snow as well; if he lives in Honolulu, where the weather is predictably good day in and day out, he is completely free to have a picnic. Where weather conditions are less predictable, the individual's freedoms which are affected by the weather will be less clear. While there may be some ambiguity, then, about freedoms which are affected by unpredictable events, it may be assumed that by and large the degree of freedom for a given behavior will be a function of what a person expects. If he expects good weather, he will feel free to have a picnic, and if he expects bad, he will feel less free to do so. His expectation, in turn, will depend upon how well he feels he understands the relevant factors which determine the event in question. On the one hand, he may have a "theory" which allows him to predict with great confidence the occurrence or non-occurrence of a particular event, while on the other hand, he may be limited to simple extrapolation into the future of what has happened in the past. If he lacks both theory and knowledge of what has happened in the past, his expectations and corresponding freedoms will be weak or non-existent.

To return to the example involving a picnic, let us assume that the individual has considerable confidence that the weather will be good on Sunday and is contemplating a picnic, but that he is actually leaning more toward attending a movie. If, then, on Sunday morning he awakens to find rain clouds in the sky, his freedom to have a picnic is surely threatened. Thus he should experience reactance, the magnitude of which would be a function of the extent of the threat and of the importance to him of this particular freedom. The effects of this reactance are readily predictable: first, the idea of having a picnic (except for rain) should increase in attractiveness; second, he can make preparations for having the picnic in spite of rain (by wearing a swimsuit, obtaining a large umbrella, or planning to have the picnic in a shelter, etc.); but in this particular case there is no obvious way in which he might attempt to re-establish his freedom by implication.

In the example we have chosen, the individual has little or no control over the event which threatens to eliminate his freedom. However, this will not always be the case, and where such control is possible, as would be the case if the individual saw nails on the road in the path of his car, we might expect that he would take the opportunity to re-establish his freedom directly, in this case by sweeping away the nails. Nevertheless, it will frequently be true of threatened natural events which would eliminate freedoms that there will be no way of intervening with the event in order to protect the freedom.

Impersonal threats to free behaviors may also arise from the actions of individuals and organizations, and what has already been said about threats from natural events would apply here as well. In addition, however, the establishment of behavioral freedoms may occur by formal or informal verbal agreement. An example of a freedom established in this way is a manufacturer's written guarantee that a product will be replaced if found defective in workmanship or materials.

A few examples of impersonal threats to freedom which originate in organizations or other persons may help to indicate the form these threats can take. When the city government considers prohibiting parking on city streets, this threatens a freedom to the automobile driver. Furthermore, unless the city is very small indeed, or unless drivers organize, the individual driver will feel that there is little which he can do to prevent this loss of freedom. Or, suppose a manufacturer withdraws a product from the market. If this product were not available from another manufacturer, then the individual's freedom to obtain that product would be threatened. And, as a final example, think of a person who is in a theater watching a movie when two people sit down behind him and commence to talk with each other rather audibly. Let us suppose that the individual is mainly killing time anyway and is therefore not particularly frustrated by not being able to hear the dialogue from the picture. Nevertheless, he should experience reactance from the disturbance because he *might* have wanted to hear the dialogue. But it should be clear that the threat to his freedom to hear the sound from the movie is quite impersonal.

An interesting feature of impersonal threats is that they will frequently be quite specific in where they apply. This, of course, is because they are not aimed at a specific person. Thus it will sometimes be possible for the individual to re-establish his freedom by moving from one place to another. In the above examples, an individual could move to another part of the country to gain the kind of weather which does not threaten freedoms important to him; a person could move to a city which did not prohibit parking on the streets; and a person could move to another seat in the theater so that the conversation would no longer be audible.

There is one further general implication in regard to impersonal threats which is interesting to note. As has been said, the sources of impersonal threats will frequently be events outside of one's own control. But since there is a dimension of control, the extent to which one has control and can wield it in the service of protecting one's freedom is a function of one's abilities, achievements, etc., which happen to be relevant to the threatening event in question. In general, the greater is a person's ability or achievement, the greater can be his freedom. Suppose, for example, that a person felt able (and therefore, in regard to an ability, free) to play nine holes of golf in about 45 strokes. But suppose further that on a given round of play, "fate" is against him such that on one occasion his ball hits a rock on the fairway and bounces into the rough, on another occasion his ball hits another ball and caroms into a water hazard, and on yet another occasion his drive off the tee catches a bird in flight and falls into deep woods. These mishaps are "threats" to his freedom to play nine holes in 45 strokes, and indeed, enough of them would certainly eliminate this freedom for the round in question. What is noteworthy, however, is that although he cannot control such mishaps, the reactance he experiences should lead him to try to improve his relevant skills, for by doing so, he can re-establish his freedom to do nine holes in 45 shots.

What a person feels free to do in terms of his own abilities and motivations may not always be an accurate estimate of reality. On occasions when he believes himself able to do something, sets out to do it, and then has unexpected difficulties, his freedom to perform the task in question will lead to (1) increased desire to be able to perform the task, (2) renewed attempts to perform well, and/or (3) attempts at more difficult tasks which, if successful, would show by implication that he could perform the easier one with which he had difficulty.

As with previously discussed implications, it has proven very difficult to find published research which might serve as tests. Some evidence is available from an experiment by Torrance and Mason (1958), the data from which were further analyzed by Torrance (1959). They studied the success of six different types of influence attempts to get USAF aircrewmen to eat emergency ration meat bars called "pemmican" while on field exercises. The types of influence included one in which there was no information or influence attempt, one in which the group leader set a good example by eating a meat bar, one in which information was given, etc. The results showed that compliance was indeed differentially affected by the different types of influence. Torrance's further analysis (1959) throws light on the factors responsible for the differential success. A measure of the subject's perceptions of the extent to which an effort was made to influence them showed that the two least successful conditions were those in which there was the greatest perceived effort to influence. When subjects were regrouped by perceived pressure, the data of Table XV were obtained. The between groups differences are reliable on every measure but "Made Sick," and they indicate that as pressure to comply increased, liking for the bars, number of bars eaten, and willingness to eat the bars in the future all decreased. Although the analysis is post hoc and correlational, there is the interesting suggestion here that the amount of compliance may actually decrease as attempted social influence increases. This effect can be viewed as consistent with reactance theory, of course, if certain assumptions are made about the subjects' prior free behaviors, the restraint against non-compliance, etc. However, there seems to be no way to make a compelling case for a reactance interpretation, and at the same time, there are other plausible interpretations. For example, if subjects thought that the amount of pressure put on them to eat the bars indicated how bad the bars must taste, the results would be neatly explained. Thus, while this experiment is interesting and may well reflect the operation of reactance, it cannot be accepted as a good test of the theory.

Another line of relevant work is a series of experiments which examines the effect of barriers on the attractiveness of goal objects

TABLE XV

Mean Indices of Influence and Compliance as a Function of Perceived Pressure to Comply[a]

|  | Liking[b] | Bars eaten | Made sick (%) | Eat in future (%) |
|---|---|---|---|---|
| No pressure | 18.32 | 8.17 | 13.9 | 65.8 |
| Low pressure | 20.94 | 6.65 | 21.5 | 44.7 |
| High pressure | 23.28 | 5.71 | 23.4 | 26.9 |

[a] Adapted from Torrance (1959).
[b] The lower the number, the greater the liking.

(Wright, 1934). We turn, therefore, to a brief consideration of barriers and then to a short description of the relevant data.

A barrier is something which impedes or resists the individual's obtaining a goal object. It may be symbolic, such as an adult's instruction to a child not to touch the stove, or it may be a physical arrangement which increases the effort required to obtain the goal object. We are here primarily concerned with physical (or at least impersonal) barriers. When a person feels free to obtain a particular goal object, the insertion of a barrier should threaten that freedom and arouse reactance in him. The greater is the barrier—i.e., the more difficulty the barrier introduces in obtaining the goal object—the greater will be the magnitude of reactance and consequent motivation to re-establish one's freedom to obtain the goal object. Since one way of re-establishing one's freedom would be to obtain the goal object despite the barrier, we might expect, considering reactance alone, that the tendency to take the goal object would be a direct function of the magnitude of the barrier. But this would ignore the effort necessary to overcome the barrier, which also increases with the magnitude of the barrier. To the extent this effort is noxious, it will reduce one's tendency to try to overcome the barrier. Thus, there is a predictive impasse in that the effects of the barrier and the consequent reactance oppose each other and it is not possible to say which, if either, will be the stronger.

It will be remembered that a similar impasse was disclosed in our analysis of social threats to freedom. If a person is told by another that he must do something, we cannot tell a priori whether the pressure to comply or the pressure to re-establish freedom will be greater. However, we can predict a change in the *relative* strength of the opposing tendencies by utilizing a variable which affects the magnitude of reactance but not its opposing tendency. In the case of physical barriers, such a variable might be the degree of importance of the prior freedom to obtain the goal object. Where, for example, the importance of one's freedom to take the goal object is relatively great, we might expect a relatively strong tendency for the individual to try to obtain the goal object if a barrier were introduced.

As the difficulty of overcoming a barrier becomes greater, a point may be reached where the individual will no longer think the goal object (and/or re-establishment of freedom) is worth the effort. Reactance can still occur under these conditions, but its effects will be subjective and, perhaps, in terms of attempts at restoration of freedom by implication.

Not all of Wright's (1934) work is relevant to the problem of impersonal barriers, and of that which is relevant, only a part yields evidence that a barrier enhances desire for the goal object. We will not attempt to describe all of this work, but rather will only indicate some interesting findings. Attempts to replicate some of Wright's findings (Child, 1946; Child and Adelsheim, 1944) and to obtain the enhancement effect with other types of barriers (Irwin, Armitt, and Simon, 1943; Irwin, Orchinik, and Weiss, 1946) have failed. Given this apparent ambiguity in results, the field experiment to be described can only be taken as illustrative of how barriers can affect behavior.

At the time of Wright's study, female students served as waitresses for other students in the women's dining hall of Duke University. Dishes of food were picked up by the waitress from a serving table three feet deep, placed on serving trays, and then carried into the dining room. The following study was concerned with how the waitresses selected items for themselves. Unknown to these waitresses, Wright arranged to have desserts placed on the pick-up surface in two rows, one close to the front (within easy reach), the other 18 inches further back (more difficult to reach). Then, when these girls picked up desserts for themselves, a tally was kept of the frequency with which they chose from the front, easy, or back, more difficult, row. These arrangements and observations were made on several different occasions. On each occasion, only one kind of dessert was served and the portions were approximately equal. In addition, the different kinds of desserts which were served on different occasions were rated for their attractiveness by the experimenter and by 10 of the girls after they had served as subjects.

Unfortunately, the evidence necessary to make a case that the subjects should have felt free to take any dessert is not available. It is plausible to assume, however, that normally, whatever desserts were put out would have been placed as conveniently as possible for the waitresses, rather than being placed so that some were distinctly more difficult to reach, and therefore that these girls had learned to expect to be able to take any dessert made available without difficulty. Thus, the placement of some desserts 18 inches back from the front row may well have been seen as a threat to their freedom to select any dessert, and we might plausibly expect to find some tendency on the part of these girls to select desserts from the more difficult row.

Our interpretation is post hoc, of course, and will necessarily fit the results. It was found that over 14 occasions on which observations were made, 60% of the choices were from the more distant row. It is also of interest that when the more attractive desserts were involved, 62% of the selections were from the back row, while only 58% were taken when the less attractive desserts were served. This difference would be expected in terms of reactance theory, of course, since the more attractive desserts would make the freedom to choose more important.

The results of other conditions showed that when the far row was only two inches back of the near row, so that there was only a minimal barrier, only 55% of selections were from the far row. On the other hand, when the far row was some 32 inches behind the near row, and very difficult to reach, only 6% of the choices came from it. Thus, when there is a negligible barrier and therefore little threat to one's freedom, there is less tendency to select the goal object with the barrier, and when the barrier becomes very large, the difficulty of obtaining the goal object may be so great that it is hardly ever selected despite whatever reactance may be aroused.

It would seem then, that this experiment by Wright can be explained in terms of reactance theory. While other of Wright's data might be similarly analyzed, it would be a more cogent test of the theory to construct an experiment along the lines of his work on barriers, but with a design capable of pinning the effect down to reactance. As a first step in this direction, the following experiment was designed and conducted by myself and Thomas Hammock.

The subjects consisted of 47 boys and 57 girls, from the first, fourth, and fifth grades of a public elementary school,[6] who were randomly assigned to either a Choice or No Choice condition. To begin with, the experimenter visited the classrooms of the subjects and told them that he would be asking each of them to leave their class briefly and play a game with him. Subjects were then individually taken to a small room in the center of which was a table approximately 2 feet wide and 6 feet long. The subject was asked to stand about six inches from one end of the table, facing it.

[6] This research was carried out at Watts Elementary School in Durham, North Carolina. The investigators wish to express their appreciation to Mr. Charles B. Whitley, Principal, and to the following teachers: Mrs. Mary M. Bates, Mrs. Hilda D. Bell, Mrs. Patricia H. Folck, Mrs. Lorraine S. Gergen, Mrs. Mary W. Harward, Mrs. Betty C. Hubbard, Miss Katherine L. Kluttz, Mrs. Margaret F. McClesky, Mrs. Kipp K. Neaves, Mrs. Gail J. Riutort, and Mrs. Gwen G. Spencer.

The procedure then consisted of asking the subject some introductory questions about his interests in order to relax him, telling him that he would receive a piece of candy, and then asking him to point to which of two pieces he thought was best, one of these pieces being near to him, the other, far. In the No Choice condition before pointing to which was best, he was given his piece of candy for doing so, while in the Choice condition he was told he could have either of the two pieces on the table for pointing to which was best. The candies were after-dinner mints which differed only in color: the two placed on the table were yellow and pink, and in the No Choice condition, the one given prior to the judgment was green. The positions of the yellow and pink mints were rotated within conditions. The instructions for the Choice condition were as follows.

"I'll bet you like candy, don't you. Would you like to have a piece of candy? (Pause for the subject's reply.) Well, I'm going to let you have a piece of candy; in fact, I'm going to let you choose between two different pieces of candy and you can have whichever one you want. I'm going to put the two different pieces of candy on the table and I want you to point to whichever piece of candy you think is the best one." The experimenter then placed one piece of candy 3 inches from the near edge of the table, the other 33 inches from the same edge. The experimenter then said, "Now, point to the piece of candy you think is the best one."

Instructions in the No Choice condition were identical except that the experimenter said, "I'm going to give you this piece of candy (the experimenter held up a green mint) if you'll tell me which of the two other pieces of candy you think is the best one. I'm going to put the two other pieces of candy on the table and I want you to point to the piece of candy you think is the best one, and then I'll give you this piece of candy (again holding the green mint)."

Let us pause a moment to consider the difference between these conditions. It must first be admitted that because the barrier is introduced by the experimenter's placing the candies near and far while the subject looks on, the barrier may be more personal than impersonal. But we will ignore this point for the moment since either type of barrier would theoretically be capable of arousing reactance. The significant difference between the conditions is that in the Choice condition the barrier threatens the subject's freedom to select whichever mint he wants, while in the No Choice condition, the subject does not have this freedom and so the barrier should have relatively little effect on which the subject thinks is best.

The results were that 25 out of 53 subjects in the No Choice condition, or 47%, said the far candy was the better. In the Choice condition, 33 out of 51, 65% of the subjects, said the far one was the better. This difference, while significant at only the 12% level, is in line with our expectations. This evidence provides some support for our contention that barriers may constitute a threat to one's freedom which in turn arouses reactance and a consequent increased desire for the item protected by the barrier.

However, aside from the low statistical reliability of the obtained effects, some additional caution should be taken in interpreting these results. In our pretesting for this project it was found that the tendency of the subject to select the far candy was affected by the behavior of the experimenter: if he was sober and businesslike, there was little tendency to select the far one, but if he was concerned and excited, selections of the far one were more frequent. We believe this was because the situation and choice had little inherent importance for the subject but could be given importance by the concerned behavior of the experimenter. Therefore, in the experiment proper the experimenter was quite animated and, of course, attempted to be just as animated in the No Choice condition as in the Choice. There is the possibility, however, that the experimenter was more animated in the Choice condition, and that this factor accounts for the obtained difference.

Of course, there are other possible explanations both for the present experiment and for the effects which Wright obtained. In sum, the data on the effect of barriers on the attractiveness of goal objects may be taken as lending some support to our analysis in terms of reactance theory, but they fall short of serving as a rigorous test.

We turn now from barriers to consideration of some other kinds of forces which may impersonally threaten one's free behaviors. It was mentioned earlier that organizations may frequently take action which threatens an individual's freedom to behave in certain ways, and commercial organizations would certainly be no exception. What may not be so obvious, however, is that acts which on their face look quite beneficial to the individual may, by virtue of threatening freedoms, have relatively negative effects. We have seen this relationship in the experiment by Brehm and Cole (1966) where it was found that a favor can decrease the likelihood of a return favor. Let us now see how a similar process may operate in regard to the less personal acts of commercial organizations.

A retail store is interested in selling its goods and, in order to promote sales, it frequently carries out promotional campaigns to increase sales of one or more products. Promotions come in a variety of forms, some of which will go unnoticed by the customer (even though they may have their intended effect) as when a product is given a more handy or prominent display, and some of which will be seen by the customer as attempts to influence him to buy. While promotional techniques such as advertising may carry useful information and convincing arguments which help to persuade people to buy, it should also be true that whenever the individual perceives that a technique is intended to influence him, his freedom not to buy that item should be threatened, as may be his freedom to buy competing items.

Just what, it may be asked, are the freedoms of the shopper and what determines their importance? Where there are competing stores and products within stores, the individual is free to select which of the competing types of necessity items he will buy, and he is free to buy or not in regard to luxuries, as well as being free to select among the competing types. The importances of these freedoms will be determined by those factors operating in any choice situation and they will not be reviewed here. However, it should be noted that competing items will frequently appear essentially identical to the consumer, particularly if he knows little about the sort of thing for which he is shopping. Under these conditions, of course, the freedom to select one rather than another would have relatively little importance.

It should be true, then, that if a consumer is exposed to a promotional message that he must buy a particular item, and if he had intentions of possibly doing otherwise, he should experience reactance. Since the threatened freedom could be directly restored by not buying the item in question, we would expect to find the individual tending to avoid buying it.

But now suppose that in addition to the message telling one to buy the particular item, some incentive were added to further encourage compliance. Typical incentives used in promotional work are reductions in price, trading stamps, coupons for free gifts, etc. It is clear that these kinds of incentives add pressure to buy the item for which they are given. At the same time, according to reactance theory, if they are seen as intended to influence the buyer's choices, they should threaten whatever freedom he feels in regard to buying the item. Thus, to the extent that this particular behavioral freedom is important to him, the buyer will experience reactance when offered an incentive to buy a particular item. The greater the importance of the freedom and/or the greater the magnitude of the incentive, the greater will be the amount of reactance aroused. Since the pressure to buy and the reactance which would lead to not buying both increase with the magnitude of the incentive, this is another case in which the resultant tendency is difficult to predict and will depend, at least in part, upon other determinants of the magnitude of reactance. However, the greater is the magnitude of an incentive, the more clearly will it be perceived as an attempt to control the buyer's behavior and thereby threaten his freedom. Thus, small incentives, which are rather common, may be seen as a gentle indication that the store would like to have the consumer buy a particular item, while a large incentive may be seen as an attempt to "force" the consumer to buy the item. While the former might be seen as "information"—i.e., then the item costs less—the latter will almost inevitably be seen as an attempt to control one's behavior and therefore a threat to one's freedom.

Verbal appeals can create similar differences in perceived force. Thus, the polite appeal, "please buy" indicates that the store would like to sell, while the more direct "buy!" is more likely to be seen as an attempt to control the shopper's behavior. Clearly, the latter would more likely be seen as a threat to any relevant freedom felt by the shopper.

This analysis of promotional techniques suggests that both verbal appeals and incentives may, if applied too strongly, lead to reactance and consequent resistance to compliance. These possibilities were investigated in the following experiment by Judith Weiner and myself.

### Buying Behavior as a Function of Verbal and Monetary Inducements

The present study was designed to threaten a shopper's freedom with both verbal and monetary inducements to buy a specific product. Whereas relatively high freedom was left to a shopper by giving him a polite request to buy the product, his freedom was threatened by instructing him that he was going to purchase the product whether he had intended to or not. To justify instructing or requesting the shopper to buy the particular product, the shopper was also always given sufficient money with which to buy it. The monetary threat to the shopper's freedom then consisted of giving him more than the price of the product he was asked or instructed to purchase.

## METHOD

The study was conducted in a supermarket in a shopping center. On Monday and Tuesday of one week premeasures were made. On the following Monday and Tuesday shoppers were randomly assigned to one of the two verbal inducement conditions and received either the price of the item or more than the price of the item. On these days from 8:30 A.M. when the store opened until approximately 12:30 P.M. when the noon lull began, a customer entering the store received a printed card requesting him to buy a specified type of bread and containing money for its purchase. On each day bread buying was observed and approximately one fourth of the shoppers were interviewed after they left the store.

### Verbal Inducement

Some cards given customers contained a statement (Low Pressure) designed to encourage the customer to purchase the bread without materially reducing his perceived choice to refuse. It read, "Today, regardless of whether or not you planned to buy bread or what kind you planned to buy, please try————(brand name) sandwich bread, king size loaf, 25¢." Other cards contained the statement (High Pressure) designed to reduce freedom. It was identical to the Low Pressure card except that it substituted "you are going to buy" for the words "please try."

### Monetary Inducement

The advocated product was a 25¢ loaf of bread. On Monday each card contained a quarter attached below the verbal inducement. On Tuesday each card contained a quarter and a dime. The extra dime was intended to be perceived as a clear attempt to "force" the shopper to comply, and thereby threaten his freedom. There appeared at the bottom of all cards the sentence, "You need not retain this card" in order to assure the customer that he could actually pocket the money and would not have to turn it in at the checkout counter.

### Assignment to Experimental Conditions

Shopping baskets bore on each side an inconspicuous but easily discernible marking of either red or green tape. The coded baskets were alternated and were kept in alternating order by a male assistant. Those customers who happened to select a green-marked basket were given the Low Pressure cards as they passed the dispensary point and those who selected red markings received High Pressure cards. Those shoppers who did not take baskets but who did pass the point where the experimenter was distributing cards were assigned alternately to one of the two conditions.

Those customers either with or without baskets who slipped into the store through the check-out lanes (in spite of our efforts to prevent their doing so) and did not pass the dispensary point did not receive cards. People who indicated that they were only accompanying a shopper did not receive cards, nor did non-basket shoppers who were, in the experimenter's estimation, under 21 years of age. All of these shoppers who did not receive a card were excluded from the analysis. Juveniles (under 21) with baskets were given cards and were eliminated from the data later, using the observer's estimate of age as the criterion.

### Card Distribution

The experimenter was dressed casually and carried a brown folder containing the cards. She was at all times pleasant and friendly. She wished the customer good morning and offered him the card. When there was any ambiguity about whether or not to give a card, she asked the customer if he was shopping, or in instances of couples or groups entering together, she asked if they were shopping singly or together. The constituents of a group of individual shoppers without baskets were each given identical cards; however, only the data of the first group member were used. Two standard replies were used by the experimenter to answer questions about the card: "The card is for you; please keep the card," or "I really don't know. I was just hired to give a card to every customer and I really don't know any more than what's on the card." If questioned about it, she explained that the sentence, "You need not retain the card" meant that, "You need not show the card to any store personnel."

### Observation[7]

Two female observers ($O_1$ and $O_2$) were stationed at the check-out counters where they were not conspicuous to incoming patrons, though they were obvious to customers who had completed their shopping. They wore street clothes and each carried a clipboard. $O_1$ was responsible for check-out lanes 1 and 2, and $O_2$ for lanes 3 and 4. Whenever possible they observed each other's lanes to provide some estimate of accuracy. For each transaction the two O's recorded on a prepared form whether or not the customer had a basket and if so its tape color the amount of each of the several kinds of bread bought, the sex, race, and approximate age of the customer, and his total expenditure.

A third female observer, $O_3$, was stationed with the experimenter at the end of the empty-basket line and across the aisle from the front of the usually inoperant fourth check-out counter. $O_3$ was responsible for assigning non-basket customers alternately to conditions. She then noted distinguishing characteristics of the customer and his assigned condition. As the customer passed through the check-out lane she noted the lane number and the customer's total expenditure. When basket customers did not pass the experimenter and consequently did not receive a card, $O_3$ followed the notation procedure for non-basket customers. When a non-basket customer who had been assigned to a condition returned and selected a basket which would have altered his condition an appropriate notation was made on $O_3$'s record. $O_3$ also recorded subjects who left the store without making a purchase. Her final responsibility was to note those customers who refused the card or returned it to the experimenter and any comments of these and other customers.

At the end of each day's operations, the cash register tape for each check-out lane was procured as a check against the records of all cash transactions by the observers.

[7]The help of our observers, Mary Lee Brehm, Caryl Anderson, and the late Kathryn Formica, and our male assistant, Norman Staples, Jr., is gratefully acknowledged.

*Interview*

A male interviewer was stationed outside the store near the exit. He made his selection of interviewees by rotating between the check-out lanes in operation and taking the first customer whose total sales he could positively identify. He generally could not identify the experimental condition of the shopper at the time of interviewing. After the customer left the store, the interviewer first asked him if he had received a card and upon an affirmative reply proceeded with the interview. He used an interview schedule but allowed himself some flexibility in order to glean maximum information.

The interview began with very general questions about what was going on in the store, and gradually focused on the specific operations of the experiment. The intention was to find out how much customers were aware of the observation and the connection between it and the bread promotion, and then to find out how customers reacted to the verbal and monetary inducements. While evidence from the interviews will be presented later, it may be noted here that customers did not connect the bread promotion and the observation, and generally did not realize there was a check to see whether or not they had bought bread and what kind they had bought.

*Compilation of Raw Data.*

Cash register tapes were checked against the records of $O_1$ and $O_2$. Common observations of the O's were matched and disagreements reconciled by assuming that they were cases of omission. The experimental condition of non-basket customers was added to $O_1$ and $O_2$'s records from those of $O_3$. If $O_3$ did not have a record of a non-basket customer, it was assumed that no card had been given him and he was deleted. Customers returning or refusing cards were placed in a special category. Exceptions to assignment of condition noted by $O_3$ were corrected and basket customers who received no card, as noted by $O_3$ were deleted. When a group of shoppers came through a check-out lane, only the first was used as a subject. One subject whom the interviewer discovered could not read was deleted. Those shoppers who might recognize any of the study personnel or their affiliation with Duke University were deleted.

Table XVI shows the remaining number of usable subjects.

TABLE XVI

NUMBER OF USABLE SUBJECTS IN EACH CONDITION

|  | Premeasure (week 1) | Low pressure (week 2) | High pressure (week 2) |
|---|---|---|---|
| Females |  |  |  |
| Monday | 61 | 41 | 40 |
| Tuesday | 68 | 32 | 34 |
| Males |  |  |  |
| Monday | 19 | 8 | 15 |
| Tuesday | 27 | 20 | 9 |

RESULTS

The observations made it possible to classify each shopper along the following dimensions: sex, white-Negro, and amount of purchases. However, sex of shoppers was the only categorization to produce a detectable effect and is the only one retained in the following presentation of results.

The shopper's behavior could be categorized into one of four classes: bought bread X (the specified item); bought bread X plus other bread; bought other bread; bought no bread. Since, if a person bought bread X *and* some other bread as well, it might mean he was complying or that he was resisting compliance, people who fell into this category were eliminated from the final analysis. There were 16 such people scattered throughout the various conditions and their inclusion would have no effect on the conclusions one might draw.

The index of primary interest is the extent to which shoppers bought bread X. An estimate of the normal proportion of shoppers buying bread X is available from the pre-experimental observations on corresponding days. Looking first at female shoppers, in Table XVII it may be seen that 23.6% on Monday, and 17.9% on Tuesday bought bread X. There is a very slight decrease in the proportion buying the critical loaf from Monday to Tuesday, but the difference is nowhere near statistical reliability ($\chi^2 = .59$). On the following Monday, when just the price of the bread was given with the verbal inducement, it was expected that the Low Pressure request to buy bread X would increase the proportion buying it, while the High Pressure insistence that one was going to buy X would produce relatively less compliance, perhaps even below

TABLE XVII

COMPLIANCE (BUYING BREAD X) AMONG FEMALE SHOPPERS

|  | Monday | | Tuesday | |
|---|---|---|---|---|
|  | N | % | N | % |
| Control (normal buying) | 55 | 23.6 | 67 | 17.9 |
|  | With 25¢ | | With 35¢ | |
|  | N | % | N | % |
| Experimental | | | | |
| Low pressure | 40 | 70.0 | 30 | 40.0 |
| High pressure | 39 | 51.3 | 30 | 40.0 |

normal buying of X. The outcome, as seen in Table XVII, shows that female shoppers exposed to the Low Pressure inducement were much more likely than normal to buy bread X, exactly 70% of them doing so. However, though the High Pressure inducement also produced a large proportion buying X (51.3%), it did not produce as much compliance as the Low Pressure approach. While the difference between the Low and High Pressure conditions might fairly easily have occurred by chance ($.10 < p < .15$), it nevertheless lends some support to our expectations that the stronger verbal inducement would arouse reactance and result in less compliance.

On Tuesday an additional dime was added to the card in order to put more pressure on customers to buy bread X, with the expectation that the additional pressure would result in less compliance. Table XVII shows that this expectation is supported strongly in the Low Pressure condition where compliance drops from Monday's 70% to Tuesday's 40%, and is supported weakly in the High Pressure condition where compliance drops from 51.3% to 40%. This decrease is reliable in the Low Pressure condition ($p < .05$), nowhere nearly reliable in the High condition, and reliable in the two conditions combined ($p < .05$). Hence, it is clear that, as expected, the additional dime *decreases* compliance among female shoppers.

The effects of the verbal and monetary inducements on male shoppers was quite different from that on the females. As may be seen in

TABLE XVIII

COMPLIANCE AMONG MALE SHOPPERS

| | Monday | | Tuesday | |
|---|---|---|---|---|
| | N | % | N | % |
| Control (normal buying) | 18 | 16.7 | 27 | 11.1 |
| | With 25¢ | | With 35¢ | |
| | N | % | N | % |
| Experimental | | | | |
| Low pressure | 8 | 37.5 | 20 | 45.0 |
| High pressure | 15 | 73.3 | 9 | 77.8 |

Table XVIII, the verbal appeal had a rather large effect, with the High Pressure form producing more compliance than the Low. On the other hand, the amount of the monetary incentive seems to have had no effect at all. While this different reaction of the males was not predicted, it is not difficult to understand in terms of our previous analysis. Males, we may assume, are less knowledgeable and discriminating about the products in a grocery store. It should be true, then, that the importance of the freedom to select one item rather than another would be less for males than for females. Thus, inducements to buy a given item would be less likely to threaten an important freedom for males, and males would therefore experience less reactance and would be more likely to comply.

The interview data add some support to the reactance interpretation of this study. For example, although few interviewees expressed strong annoyance about either the verbal inducement or the money, there was a tendency among those who did not buy bread X for those in the High Pressure condition to report more annoyance with both the verbal message and money than those in the Low Pressure condition. In addition, while the most frequent view was that "It is just another advertising scheme," and nothing to get excited about, three of the interviewed shoppers said outright that they did not like to be told what to buy. This, it should be recalled, is despite the fact that customers were given the money with which to buy the bread.

In summary, this study lends some support to reactance theory in that it shows that monetary inducements, and probably verbal inducements, too, can result in less compliance as their strength increases. And while it is undoubtedly possible to construct alternative interpretations for the obtained results, it must not be forgotten that the obtained negative effects on compliance were predicted.

## Summary

We have tried to show that impersonal events may threaten an individual's behavioral freedoms. These threats occur through impending events which would eliminate a freedom, or through the actual occurrence of events which lead to pressures toward elimination of a freedom. The reactance that results from these threats will lead to increased desire to engage in the threatened behavior, actual attempts to engage in the threatened behavior, and, where possible, attempts to engage in behaviors which will restore one's freedom by implication. Since impersonal threats to freedom are frequently specific to a location, re-establishment of freedom can sometimes be accomplished by moving to another location. Attempts to re-establish freedom by control of the threatening event will sometimes be possible and will be a function of one's relevant abilities and skills. Thus, reactance may lead to attempts to improve one's abilities and skills in order to re-establish one's behavioral freedom.

A brief analysis of barriers indicated that they are capable of arousing reactance. Published research lends some support to this analysis in that barriers have sometimes been found to enhance one's desire for the goal object. An experiment specifically designed to see if enhancement could be attributed to reactance gave some indication that enhancement occurs to the extent that the barrier interferes with freedom to obtain the goal object. The evidence, however, was not considered unequivocally in support of reactance theory.

Finally, it was suggested that impersonal threats to freedom such as verbal appeals and monetary inducements can arouse reactance and thereby minimize compliance. A field experiment was described which obtained decreases in compliance in buying behavior with increases in strength of verbal and monetary inducements, thus lending further support to the reactance view.

# CHAPTER VI

# Persuasion and Attitude Change

In a sense a person is free to think whatever he likes. This is because, at least to date, there is no general way to monitor his thoughts except by his voluntary disclosure of them. It is also because there is no necessary connection between thought and overt behavior. If an individual wants to believe he can fly, he is free to do so as long as he keeps the thought to himself and as long as the thought does not interfere with his adjustment to his environment—that is, as long as the thought does not lead him to try a test flight off a cliff.

This relatively great degree of objective freedom of thought is not necessarily condoned by other people and social organizations. Parents attempt to instill in their children some kinds of thoughts and they attempt to stamp out others. Religious organizations prefer people to have certain theistic and moral beliefs and not others, advertising agencies want their people to believe in the products which they are promoting, and nations want citizens to agree with national policy and not to have subversive thoughts. How successful these attempts are in the control of thought is difficult to assess, but we may assume that they work to some degree. After all, there are such things as blushing and guilty looks without apparent cause, and these presumably reflect transgressions of restrictions of thought. A belief system which includes an omniscient agent, of course, has some advantage for thought control.

Although feelings, such as likes and dislikes, are not much more public than thoughts, they are more likely to have an involuntary effect on overt behavior. Perhaps for this reason, or perhaps because feelings are simply seen as more important than mere thoughts, there is even sharper delineation by other people and organizations about what one should feel. In the United States, for example, one must love his parents, his spouse, and his children and one must dislike slothfulness and poverty. The individual who appears to deviate from these prescriptions is generally viewed with suspicion and hostility.

Since we assume that there is a rather large range of thoughts and feelings which other people or organizations attempt to control, it may be asked if there are thoughts and feelings which are free to the individual. It is suggested here that there are, and that they may be roughly defined as opinions and attitudes. In general, when one perceives that it is difficult or impossible to establish the objective truth of a matter, or when one perceives that there is relatively wide disagreement among people about what one should think or feel, then one will feel free to select one's own position and/or feeling.

What the person feels free to do is adopt or not any of the distinguishably different positions on the issue. By definition, it is implied that when one position is selected, others are given up or rejected. At a minimum, of course, it must be possible to distinguish two positions, while the maximum number of positions distinguishable will depend upon the complexity of the issue and the articulation of this complexity by the individual. Complex issues may frequently be seen in terms of two or just a few positions.

The importance of the freedom to take a given position is a direct function of how closely that position represents what one believes to be correct. Thus, the greatest importance would be attached to the preferred position, the next greatest importance to the position which most closely approximated the preferred position, etc. This relationship may be seen in Fig. 1, in which the solid line represents the relationship between position and importance of the freedom to take that position. As this makes clear, the more a position deviates from the preferred one, the less is the importance of the freedom to select it. The linear slopes are not meant to indicate that these functions will necessarily be linear, though it is expected that they would be monotonically decreasing on each side of the preferred position. Fig. 1 also shows that the importance of the freedom not to take a position increases monotonically as the position deviates from the preferred one. It is a corollary that the difference in importance of freedom of adjacent positions is a direct function of how different those positions appear to the individual: if little difference is seen between two positions, there will be little difference in the importance of the freedom to adopt them.

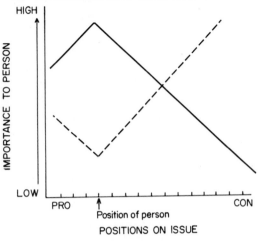

POSITIONS ON ISSUE

—— *Freedom to adopt position*

— — *Freedom not to adopt position*

FIG. 1.   The importance to the individual of the freedom to adopt or not adopt positions discrepant from the one he prefers.

Of course neither the freedom to adopt the preferred position nor the freedom to avoid adopting the most discrepant position need have much importance to the individual, and this would be reflected in a downward shift of the functions in Fig. 1. Whether or not these behavioral freedoms have importance will depend upon whether or not they are closely tied to important values which the individual holds. For example a person may think gray is the most attractive interior color for a building, but the freedom to hold this position may have little importance to him because it has little bearing on matters of consequence to him. On the other hand, the freedom to hold one's preferred political position or one's attitude toward birth control may be of great importance because they have implications for how one believes significant aspects of social life should be ordered.

It is probably not possible to eliminate the freedom to have a particular thought. But just as attempts are made to control what a person is free to think, so attempts may be made to eliminate the freedom to have a particular thought. And just as attempts at control probably have some success, so attempts at elimination may constitute threats to one's freedom. It seems likely that the same factors which make for more or less control of thought would also be those which determine whether or not attempted elimination of freedom of thought will constitute a threat.

It seems plausible to assume that some of the factors which control positive social influence also affect threat to freedom of thought. Put another way, if the communicator is one whom the individual cannot ignore on the issue in question, then the communicator has the capability of threatening the freedom of the individual to select his own position. Thus, a communicator who is expert on the issue and who is trustworthy as well should have more power to threaten one's freedom than a communicator who lacks either or both of these virtues. Similarly, a communicator who has power over one in other respects, may thereby have some potential for threatening one's freedom on opinions.

This formulation will by now have become familiar to the reader: the greater is the pressure to change in a given way, the greater is the potential threat to one's freedom and hence, the greater is the magnitude of reactance. In regard to persuasive communications and attitude change, however, there is the additional factor of the content of the communication. The content may include facts and arguments which are in themselves quite convincing and conducive to change in one's attitude in the direction advocated. But to the extent that it is perceived by the individual that the communicator is trying to make him change, his freedom to decide for himself will be threatened and he will experience reactance. Thus, there is a crucial distinction between the communicator's offering information and arguments which may help the individual to decide upon his own position, and the communicator's attempting to get the individual to adopt a particular position. Information and arguments can be quite helpful to the individual and may result in positive influence, but the perception that the communicator is attempting to influence will tend to be seen as a threat to one's freedom to decide for oneself.

There are undoubtedly many factors which contribute to the perception that the communicator is attempting to influence one, and several of these have been shown to be inversely related to attitude change. Aside from the obvious device of drawing a strong conclusion, the communicator may give a one-sided message or an emotional or extreme message, or he may be untrustworthy in that he apparently has something to gain by getting the individual to adopt his position. Simply by taking and defending a given position on the issue, the communicator may be perceived as trying to influence.

When a person experiences reactance from having his freedom to adopt his own opinion threatened, he will attempt to re-establish his freedom by *not* taking the position advocated by the communicator. He may conceivably re-establish his freedom by maintaining his original position on the issue, although we might expect that he would at least show some increased confidence that this position is correct. He can more clearly re-establish his freedom to take his own position by moving away from the position advocated by the communicator. Thus, despite the pressure to change toward the position advocated by the communicator, we can expect that when important freedoms of position are threatened, the individual will tend to show boomerang attitude change.

The testing of implications from reactance theory for the understanding of attitude change has one complication over tests in other problem areas which have been discussed. The typical experiment on attitude change utilizes attitudinal dimensions which exist apart from the experimental situation. This is because attitudes are conceptualized as relatively stable predispositions toward objects or events, and important attitudes would presumably be difficult to create experimentally. Furthermore, theories of attitude change have generally specified that persuasion will be effective under conditions where the attitude is important to the individual, or that persuasion will be effective where the individual has no strong involvement in the issue. Neither condition satisfies the requirements for a clear test of reactance implications. Rather, it is necessary that the individual consider the freedom to adopt *different* positions important, which means that while he may be on one side of an issue, he should also consider it quite possible that he might want to be on the other side or at least adopt a different position on the same side. Furthermore, to attribute attitude change effects to reactance it would be desirable to show that they vary with the freedom to adopt one's own position. As has been noted, freedom of thought is difficult to control and in regard to naturalistic attitudinal issues has been established over a long period of time and would not be easy to change. Thus, the best demonstration of the effects of reactance on attitude change as a function of persuasion would involve not only creating the attitudinal issue in the laboratory, but also creating differential amounts of freedom of thought in regard to that issue. Since this rather ambitious project has not yet been attempted, we must content ourselves with less direct evidence that reactance affects attitude change. Let us begin by examining a number of published studies which show that the perceived intent to influence results in reduced attitude change.

An experiment by Allyn and Festinger (1961) exposed subjects to a persuasive communication in disagreement with their private views under two different conditions. In one condition, subjects were asked to pay attention to the personality of the speaker while he talked and were given no warning of the stand which the speaker would take, while in the other condition, subjects were informed of the strong stand which the speaker would take. An opinion measure administered two weeks prior to the communication and immediately afterward served to assess opinion change. The results showed that there was somewhat less change in the condition in which subjects had been forewarned of the speaker's stand. Furthermore, the difference between conditions was more marked for subjects who were initially most opposed to the speaker's position. A measure was also taken of the perceived fairness of the communication, and this measure revealed that a greater proportion of those who were forewarned perceived bias in the communication. Allyn and Festinger were interested in the possibility that forewarned subjects were avoiding dissonance, and the above results are consistent with this view. They also note, however, that their view would lead one to expect that among subjects exposed to the condition of forewarning, those initially more opposed to the stand of the communicator should have had a relatively great tendency to see the communication as biased compared to those with more moderate initial positions. However, this did not turn out to be the case. There was no difference in perceived bias of the communication as a function of initial position. This result, it should be noted, is quite consistent with a reactance analysis of the experiment. The forewarning of the communicator's stand serves to threaten the subjects' freedom to decide for themselves. The amount of reactance experienced, and the consequent tendency not to change in the direction advocated, would increase with increasing discrepancy between the subject's position and the advocated one. Thus, reactance theory would lead one to expect less attitude change in the forewarned condition, and that this effect would be greater for those with relatively extreme initial positions in opposition to the communicator. Furthermore, according to the reactance view, the perceived bias of the communication is not a dependent effect but rather a part of the precondition for the arousal of reactance. Thus, perceived bias would not be expected to differ as a function of the subject's initial position. However, no claim can be made that this reactance interpretation of the experiment is uniquely adequate and we will not dwell on it further.

That the perceived intent to influence must occur prior to the persuasive communication in order to reduce persuasion effectively has been shown by Kiesler and Kiesler (1964). Using a written communication, they showed that if a footnote which indicates the message is intended to make readers change their opinions appears at the beginning of the communication, there is less opinion change than if the footnote appears at the end. This effect is not surprising, of course, since we might expect that the forewarning would facilitate the perception that the communication itself was a threat to one's opinion freedom. But it is also reported that there is no difference in opinion change between subjects who read the warning after the communication and those who received no warning at all (but read the communication), and this could be embarrassing for reactance theory. For if the perceived intent to influence is supposed to threaten one's opinion freedom and thereby arouse reactance and a tendency to disagree with the advocated position, then the warning that a communication is intended to make one change his mind should reduce the effectiveness of a communication regardless of when it appears. However, for the after-warning condition to produce less opinion change than the no-warning condition, it must be assumed that subjects in the latter perceived less intent to influence than subjects in the former. Since Kiesler and Kiesler report no data on this assumption, let us inspect their experiment somewhat more closely to see whether or not it is plausible. First of all, the description of the communication says in part, ". . . a one-sided communication advocating, in an extreme and emotional manner, . . ." From this description we may plausibly assume that subjects did not need an explicit warning in order to perceive the communication as an attempt to make them change their minds. Thus, subjects in the no-warning condition, by the time they had finished reading the communication, would have perceived the communication as a threat to their opinion freedom and would have experienced reactance. Consistent with this assumption is the fact that even in the no-warning condition there is only slightly more than two points of change on the 16-point scale. Although we cannot be

sure since before scores were not reported, it seems likely that subjects'
positions on the issue concerning foreign aid were probably relatively
moderate and not very resistant to change. The relatively small amount
of change produced may then be taken as some evidence that even the
no-warning condition aroused reactance and consequent resistance to
influence. Thus, there is no basis on which we might expect greater
reactance arousal in the after-warning condition than in the no-warning
condition: by the time the communication was completed, it was
already quite obvious to the subjects in both conditions that influence
was being attempted.

There is one further result of interest in this experiment, although
it is not statistically reliable. The mean opinion change of subjects in
the forewarned condition is *less* than that of control subjects who read
an irrelevant communication. While this effect is significant at only
about the 12% level, it was not expected by the investigators. But as we
have seen in our earlier discussion, the clearest way for a person to
re-establish his freedom to select his own opinion is by moving *away*
from the advocated position. That this movement away occurs despite
the apparent persuasiveness of the communication, as seen in the
after- and no-warning conditions, is striking indeed and may be taken
as further support of the contention that reactance is involved.

That a strongly persuasive communication informs the audience of
the communicator's intent to influence has also been noted by
Festinger and Maccoby (1964). They point out that the results of the
Allyn and Festinger (1961) experiment, which we discussed earlier,
may have been due not so much to the forewarning, since the persuasive
attempt would have tended to nullify it, but rather to the distraction
in the other condition of paying attention to the speaker's personality.
This distraction, they say, may tend to prevent the listener from
thinking of counterarguments and derogating the speaker. Three
experiments are then reported by Festinger and Maccoby in which a
persuasive communication against college fraternities was presented
in a movie to audiences of fraternity men. In one condition, the movie
showed the speaker giving the talk. In the other condition, the movie
presented an irrelevant and entertaining picture about a painter while
the soundtrack carried the persuasive talk. A post-movie measure of
attitudes toward fraternities revealed that in two of the three experiments, those presented with the "distraction" form were somewhat
persuaded while those presented with the straight form were not.

A measure of "rejection of the speaker" which combined perceptions of how well qualified he was and how fair his presentation was provided corresponding evidence that distraction tended to reduce rejection. In the third experiment groups of non-fraternity men were also shown the straight and distracting forms of the movie communication, and there it was found that the two forms produced about the same amount of positive influence. In short, the various results are clearly in line with the argument of Festinger and Maccoby that distraction tends to prevent implicit counter argument, etc., during the talk.

While a reactance interpretation of these data is perhaps no more compelling than the interpretation offered by these investigators, it handles the data just as well. It is assumed, of course, that the straight version of the movie which was a rather strongly persuasive communication, threatened the opinion freedom of the subjects. Since the freedom not to take the advocated position was more important to the fraternity members than the independents, we would expect that the straight version of the film would tend to produce more reactance and more tendency not to be persuaded among the fraternity members than among the independents.

We must also assume that the distraction movie raised questions in the minds of the subjects about what was going on. While we are not told by the report how subjects were obtained or for what they volunteered, it is clear that they were told the film was about fraternities and that it was rather unusual. Thus, since the distraction version was a little bizarre instead of being a simple anti-fraternity talk, the subjects would have been less likely to perceive the intention of the movie (and talk) as an attempt to influence them. And, of course, this is what the data on the rejection of the speaker indicate: less rejection (including less bias) in the distraction condition than in the straight. With less perceived attempt to influence there would have been less threat, consequent reactance, and resultant tendency to disagree with the advocated position. These experiments on distraction, then, may be interpreted as support for another form of the hypothesis that perceived intent to influence arouses reactance.

Actually, although the Kiesler and Kiesler (1964) experiment would seem to have provided relevant data, another experiment has been performed to show that forewarning of the position of the communicator does result in resistance to change. In addition, this experiment, by Freedman and Sears (1965), was designed to examine the distraction hypothesis of Festinger and Maccoby (1964) as well. High school teenagers were exposed to a persuasive communication about why teenagers should not be allowed to drive. Introductory instructions warned subjects either 10 minutes prior to the talk, or immediately prior to it, that the communicator would take a position against teenage driving. However, some were told to pay attention to the talk while others were told to pay attention to the personality of the speaker. In addition, there was one condition in which those told to pay attention to the talk were given a 2-minute warning about the position of the speaker in order to determine the effect of having only a short period of forewarning. The resulting opinion change indicated that the 10-minute warning group showed less persuasion in the advocated direction than did the no-warned [sic] group. On the other hand, the instruction to pay attention to either the content or the personality had only a marginally reliable effect, but this effect was in the expected direction of more change in the distraction (personality) condition. Change in the 2-minute warning condition was between that of the 10-minute condition and the no-warning condition but was nowhere nearly reliably different from either. Finally, a measure of perceived communicator bias revealed no reliable differences between conditions. While it might be thought that no differences among conditions in perceived communicator bias is evidence contrary to a reactance theory interpretation of the attitude change results, it should be noted that the question used, "How biased do you think the speaker was?" quite literally does not refer to intent to influence. A speaker can easily be seen as biased without being seen as intending to influence. Indeed, this would presumably be the normal explanation for disagreements of opinion in informal conversation. On the other hand, previous measures of rejection of the communicator or communication which have been used as evidence for perceived intent to influence have referred to unfairness, one-sidedness, or bias, in the communication itself—relatively clear indicators from the subjects' point of view of intent to influence.

Strictly speaking, this experiment by Freedman and Sears cannot be interpreted solely in terms of reactance theory. While the instruction to pay attention to the personality of the speaker would reduce the tendency to perceive the talk (and experimental session) as an attempt to make the subject change his mind, as has been noted, the effect one might expect from giving the forewarning of the communicator's stand either 10 minutes prior to the talk or only immediately prior is not completely clear. It is plausible to assume that the earlier forewarning gives the subject a greater chance to perceive that the intention of the communicator is to influence him and that it is this differential clarity of the communicator's intention which accounts for the difference between the 10-minute and no-warning conditions. But there is little to recommend this assumption aside from the fact that it makes the data explainable in terms of reactance theory. Thus, while these data are interpretable in terms of reactance theory, they do not provide strong support.

It may be noted in passing that two additional experiments concerning forewarning fail to produce reactance effects. McGuire and Papageorgis (1962), while finding that forewarning of an attack on one's position strengthened the effectiveness of preparatory defenses, also found that the forewarning did not reduce the effect of an attack when there were no preparatory defenses. It appears, however, that subjects in their unwarned condition would typically have been warned of the impending attack because they were exposed to attacks on other issues. This, of course, would tend to reduce any difference between the unwarned and forewarned conditions in the amount of reactance that might be aroused. In any case, the difference between conditions could not unambiguously be interpreted in terms of "intent to influence" since subjects in the "unforewarned" condition were given to believe they were taking a test of analytic thinking ability. Since a set to take this kind of test could affect the subjects' reactions to the measures of his position and to the communications, there is no unambiguous baseline against which to compare any possible reactance effect from the "forewarned" condition. Similarily, it is plausible to assume that subjects' reactions in the experiment by McGuire and Millman (1965) were predominantly a function of their set to do well on the "test of analytic thinking ability" and would not therefore reflect effects of reactance from the forewarning of attack on their opinion positions.

To this point we have been asserting that various kinds of experimental manipulations affect the perceived intent to persuade, and that it is the threat from this to one's opinion freedom which gives rise to reactance and a consequent tendency to disagree with the advocated position. We have seen in previous chapters that threats to freedom tend to result in attempts at restoration of freedom. However, in the present chain of logic we have not yet shown that the perceived intent to influence per se constitutes a threat to freedom. While we have no evidence to demonstrate this direct relationship, there is a report in the literature which bears on this problem. This is a report of two experiments by Walster and Festinger (1962) which demonstrate the persuasive effectiveness of overheard communications. Let us therefore examine these experiments.

The purpose was to see whether or not "overheard" persuasive communications produce more positive attitude change than do equivalent communications delivered directly. In the first experiment, introductory psychology students, as part of their course, were taken in small groups on a tour of the social psychology research laboratory observation room. In the course of this tour they were led to believe that they wouldd be able to do some "blind listening" to a conversation between two graduate students. What this actually consisted of was listening to a previously prepared and tape-recorded conversation in which the speakers discussed the "misconception" that smoking causes lung cancer. However, the subjects were led to believe that the conversation was spontaneous and occurring at the moment they were listening. Some of these subjects were also led to believe that the graduate students knew they were listening, while others were led to believe that the graduate students had no idea they were listening. A postexperimental measure of subjects' attitudes concerning the link between smoking and lung cancer revealed that those subjects who "overheard" the persuasive communication showed more positive change than those who thought their presence was known to the communicators. In addition, it was found that the difference in effectiveness of overheard and non-overheard communications was somewhat greater among smokers than among non-smokers. It had not been anticipated that the difference would be in this direction since the communication favored smoking and it was thought that smokers would change more even in the non-overheard condition. Thus, these investigators conducted a second experiment in order to find out if involvement in the issue would again have a similar effect.

The second experiment utilized two issues and two subject populations such that for one population, one issue was involving while the other was not, and for the other population, the involving and uninvolving issues were reversed. Again the subjects were led to believe either that their presence was known to the communicators or that their presence was unknown (and they were "overhearing" the message). The results of this second experiment confirmed the earlier findings: for non-involved subjects there was little or no difference in opinion change as a function of whether or not the communication was overheard, while among involved subjects, the overheard communications were clearly more effective than were the non-overheard ones. It should be noted that as in the first experiment, involvement also means agreement with the advocated position.

Walster and Festinger argue that the results cannot be accounted for by the fact that the listeners' defenses are not prepared (the explanation utilized in several of the previous experiments we have reviewed). They point out that there was no obvious attempt to influence the audience, and that in addition, why would the major resistance to the influence appear among those who agreed with the advocated position? Neither, they argue, can it be said that an overheard communication is more powerful simply because the listener is not supposed to hear it. Otherwise, they continue, the effect should have been as great for non-involved subjects as for involved. Finally, they say they are driven to the position that "Because the speaker does not know the listener is there, the speaker cannot be seen as intending to influence the listener." At the same time, however, they do not understand ". . . why, when involved subjects hear a communication which advocates a position they would like to accept, they still tend to impute ulterior motives to the speaker when this is at all possible."

An analysis in terms of reactance theory would follow the argument of Walster and Festinger quite closely. As they say, "Let us look at our experimental conditions and examine to what extent it would be possible, in any of them, to impute 'intention to influence' to the speaker. First of all, let us dispose of the overheard conditions. Clearly, since the speaker does not know anyone is listening, it is not conceivable that the listener, knowing this, could imagine that the speaker intends to influence him. In the Regular condition, however, the situation is a little different. Here the speaker knows that someone is listening but does not know who. Since the listener in the Regular condition knows he has not been personally identified by the speaker, if the content of the communication is not personally relevant, it would also seem quite difficult to imagine that the speaker was intending to influence him. If, however, the content of the communication in the Regular condition is of direct personal relevance, then it is possible for the listener to feel that the speaker is, indeed, attempting to influence him and has ulterior motives." Except for their attribution of "ulterior motives," their analysis seems appropriate for our own purposes. The apparent intention to influence would seem to account for the differential amounts of attitude change which occurred. Furthermore, viewed from reactance theory, there is nothing surprising about the fact that people show a tendency to disagree with the advocated position even when they are presumably on the same side of the issue. For even though the importance of the freedom not to take the advocated position should not be very great, there is still a threat to freedom of opinion in the "intent to influence." In addition, it may also be noted that one of the two issues in the second experiment produced a boomerang effect. While this effect is not statistically reliable, it can be considered noteworthy since, as in former cases we have discussed, it occurs despite a persuasive communication in the opposite direction. And such an effect is, of course, completely consistent with our interpretation in terms of reactance theory.

The notion that the perceived intention of the communicator to influence would be a factor controlling effectiveness of the communication is not new. For example, Hovland, Janis, and Kelley in their volume *Communication and Persuasion* (1953) devote several pages of discussion to this possibility. Their emphasis, however, is upon the effect which intent to influence would have on the informational value of the communication and upon the positive and negative emotional and motivational components which lead to acceptance or rejection of the message. Thus, they would expect that the perception of intent to influence would tend to make one doubt that the communicator's communication was fair and unbiased, and it would arouse feelings of suspicion, etc., which tend to interfere with acceptance of the communication.

As we have seen, the analysis of the attitude change paradigm in terms of reactance theory emphasizes the perceived intent to influence as a threat to one's freedom to make up one's own mind. Thus, whatever factors promote the perception that the communicator is attempting influence may also arouse reactance and a consequent tendency to disagree with the advocated position. For example, the perception that the communicator has something to gain by having his audience accept a certain position, the perception that the communicator is purposely leaving out crucial facts or arguments, the perception that the communicator is trying "too hard" to make his case, etc., would tend to give rise to the perception of intent to influence.

But whether or not significant amounts of reactance will be aroused by the perceived intent to influence depends in turn upon whether or not the individual feels he is free to make up his own mind on the issue, and whether or not the freedoms to take or not take different positions are important to him. It is therefore not appropriate to say that an obvious intention to influence will always meet with resistance and failure. Only when important freedoms are threatened would we expect boomerang attitude change from an obvious influence attempt.

Reports by Mills and Aronson (1965) and Mills (1966) show that under some conditions an intent to influence can facilitate positive attitude change. The former study showed that when the communicator states he would like to influence others, the tendency to adopt his position increases as his attractiveness increases. The second study showed that when the communicator states he would like to influence others, the tendency to adopt his position is increased by the perception that he likes the communicatee, and decreased by the perception he dislikes the communicatee. Both of these studies were carried out with issues of low importance to the subjects and we may assume that reactance arousal was therefore minimal.

In several of the experiments we have described, in which either forewarning of the communicator's position or distraction from the communication were shown to affect attitude change, the investigators suggested that the mechanism by which resistance against change occurs is implicit counterargument and derogation of the communication and communicator. As we have tried to show, the view in terms of reactance theory does not necessitate any such mechanisms since the arousal of reactance will lead to a tendency to disagree with the communicator whether one can counterargue or not. Given an issue on which a person feels he has opinion freedoms of some importance, all that should be necessary to produce "resistance" to change, or even boomerang change, is a clear pressure on the individual to change. It is well known, of course, that such pressure can be contained in the information about the position of another, comparable, person. The more, within limits, the position of a comparable person is discrepant from one's own, the greater is the pressure on oneself to change toward the other person's position. Now if one learns the position of another in an incidental manner, then there should be no perception that one is being subjected to an influence attempt. However, if one is told that one is expected to be positively influenced by learning the position of another, then one's opinion freedom would be clearly threatened, and he should experience reactance. We shall now describe an experiment designed and conducted by myself and Karalyn Krasin, which was specifically intended to show that the "resistance" effect from perceived intent to influence can occur in the *absence* of a persuasive communication, that is, a communication which includes facts and arguments against which one may implicitly counterargue.

The subjects consisted of freshman girls from a single dormitory at Duke University. They were individually contacted by the experimenter and asked to fill out an opinion questionnaire for the Psychology Department. On the following day, each was again contacted and was asked to predict the position of another person on certain items on the questionnaire on the basis of that person's answers to the other items, and they were also requested to indicate again their own opinions on the issues. However, a random selection of the subject population was also told, as will be explained below, that their answers were expected to move toward agreement with those of the student whose opinions were already marked on the questionnaire.

The questionnaire contained 12 opinion statements on unrelated topics such as federal subsidization of fine arts and abolishment of capital punishment. Each statement was accompanied by a row of members running from $-5$ to $+5$, with the former labeled "disagree strongly," and the latter labeled "agree strongly." There was no zero or neutral point. Instructions at the beginning of the questionnaire explained that answers would be kept completely confidential and were to be used for research purposes only. The subject was asked to read each statement and circle the number which best represented his position on the issue.

Prior to a second contact with the subject, a questionnaire was prepared for him. A position was circled on the response scale for each item except items six and twelve. The positions circled were arranged so that they would agree with the subject's initial position on some items, but on others they would disagree by 1, 2, or 3 scale positions on the 10-point scale, always in the direction of the opposite end of the scale. The discrepancy sizes were systematically varied so that a given item did not always have the same size discrepancy.

When the student was contacted the second time, she was told:

"This study was given to students in an eastern university. The answers of one student are given for questions 1 through 5 and 7 through 11. First, read this student's opinions for questions 1 through 5; then try to predict how he would answer question 6. Then read his opinions for questions 7 through 11 and try to predict how he would answer question 12 . . . Next, go back with the pencil and fill in your own opinions again for all 12 questions." This was the complete set of instructions for the Low Threat condition. The instructions for the High Threat condition were identical but added, "We are sure you will be greatly influenced by the opinions stated, and that your answers this time will tend toward those of this student." The second questionnaire was anonymous in both conditions.

Thus, in the Low Threat condition, subjects were led to believe that they were shown the other student's position only so they could try to predict his position on two of the issues. High Threat subjects also thought they were given the information for this purpose, but they were also informed that they were expected to show opinion change in the direction of the other person's position. We would expect, of course, that the latter condition would threaten the subjects' freedom to adopt their own positions on the issues, and that consequently they would experience reactance and tend to disagree. Since the pressure to change should be a direct function of the discrepancy size, in the Low Threat condition there should be increased opinion change with increased discrepancy. But in the High Threat condition, the magnitude of reactance should increase as discrepancy and pressure increase. Thus, any increase in opinion change from low to high discrepancy should be less in the High than in the Low Threat condition. If relatively important freedoms were threatened by this pressure to change, it could be expected that as discrepancy size increased, opinion change would tend to become increasingly negative.

The mean opinion change scores are shown in Table XIX. They support the expectation that in the Low Threat condition, increases in discrepancy would result in increases in amount of opinion change. Also as expected, the effect of discrepancy size on change is quite different in the High Threat condition: as discrepancy size increases, opinion change first becomes less positive and then becomes slightly negative. The interaction between discrepancy sizes 1 and 3 and Threat conditions is significant at better than the 5% level by analysis of variance. Thus, the results rather clearly support our expectations.

TABLE XIX

MEAN OPINION CHANGE AS A FUNCTION OF THREAT AND DISCREPANCY

| | Discrepancy Size | | | |
|---|---|---|---|---|
| | 0 | 1 | 2 | 3 |
| Low threat ($N = 9$) | $-.22^a$ | .15 | .50 | .57 |
| High threat ($N = 13$) | $-.17$ | .07 | .00 | $-.13$ |

[a] A minus sign indicates movement away from the position of the other person. Only minus change is possible where the discrepancy size is zero.

This study does not rule out the possibility that people do implicit counterarguing while listening to a persuasive communication, nor does it even rule out the possibility that implicit counterargument occurred in the present experiment. But the latter possibility is not very plausible as the factor which accounts for the reduced and even negative change in the High Threat condition. Since there were several issues, and since subjects spent only a few minutes filling out the questionnaire, they were not likely to be implicitly counterarguing on each one. It seems more plausible to assume that they were simply motivated to disagree with the intended influence.

### The Direct Attempted Elimination of Opinion Freedom

Aside from the fact that it would be somewhat unusual, there is no reason why a communicator who delivers a persuasive message should not make a direct attempt to eliminate the opinion freedom of his audience. That is, after the delivery of a communication on the issue, the communicator may conclude by telling his audience that they have no choice but to agree with him. Although this type of attempted elimination of freedom would not normally occur in real life, it should serve as a test for our understanding of how reactance affects opinions.

While the unusualness of this approach attests to the fact that it may be bad practice for someone studied in the arts of persuasion, it also suggests that questions may be raised in the minds of those exposed to such an approach about various aspects of the communicator and his message. For example, the attempted elimination of freedom could reduce the perceived trustworthiness or expertness of the communicator, or it might produce the perception that the communicator is extreme or fanatical. Similarly, the communication might be seen as more one-sided or less fair, or the communicator's conclusion might be seen as unwarranted, when he attempts to eliminate the freedom of his audience. These factors, it will be clear, could also lead to less effectiveness of the persuasive attempt and would therefore tend to confound an interpretation in terms of reactance theory. Thus, the experiments to be described attempted to measure a variety of perceptions of the communicator and communication in order to check on such alternative possibilities.

The first experiment, designed and carried out by Mary L. Brehm, was intended to show that when the communicator attempts to eliminate the freedom of his audience to draw their own conclusions, members of the audience will experience reactance and a consequent tendency to disagree with the communicator's conclusion. The procedure was as follows.

The experimenter entered a large lecture course in psychology[8] and asked the students to fill out an opinion questionnaire, ostensibly as part of a larger study of student opinions on issues related to education. It was explained that the questionnaires were anonymous but that each had a code number, and the students were asked to copy off the code number and keep it with them for the next few weeks so that the same number could be used in further projects of the research program.

The questionnaire contained statements of 12 issues related to education and campus affairs. Each item was accompanied by a 61-point scale marked at 10-point intervals with verbal labels running from "Favor Extremely" to "Against Extremely," and with the midpoint marked "Neither." Under each opinion scale was a 31-point Importance scale, with labels running from "None" to "Great." Thus, for each issue there was a measure of where the individual stood and how important the issue was to him.

Among the 12 items on the questionnaire was the one which pretesting had indicated would be suitable for the experiment. That is, opinions on this issue were divided, they were not extreme, and the issue was of moderate importance. It was therefore assumed that subjects would feel some freedom of opinion on the issue, that these relevant freedoms would have some importance to them, and their

[8]The help of Professors Jay Birnbrauer, William Hopkins, and Herbert Wells is gratefully acknowledged.

positions would not be so strong that reactance effects could not be shown. The item was, "De-emphasis of intercollegiate athletics."

A week after the administration of the pre-questionnaire, the experimenter again entered the class and announced that she was gathering some further information. She explained that she wanted to get their reactions to a statement on one of the issues included in the previous questionnaire, that each student would be given a copy of the statement and an attached questionnaire, and that they should first read the statement and then answer the questions which followed.

The experimental materials consisted of a cover sheet which asked for the student's code number and sex, a communication, and a questionnaire. Unknown to the subjects, two forms of the communication were passed out alternately among them. This was possible since the two forms were identical except that one contained a final sentence which the other did not. The written introduction for the communication said:

"As part of a nation-wide study of student opinions sponsored by the National Education Research Council, a meeting of students was held in Chicago in October, 1962. Representatives from 52 selected state and private schools attended. The purpose of the meeting was to debate various topics involving campus activities related to education. One of the topics discussed was whether intercollegiate athletics should be de-emphasized.

"Mr. John Marstow, a student at the University of Colorado, made the following statement regarding this issue."

The communication was a two-paragraph statement designed to appear well-reasoned, two-sided, and non-emotional, but which in sum argued strongly in favor of intercollegiate athletics. It concluded: "In summary, there are great advantages in the development of a large and active program in intercollegiate athletics. I conclude that, if anything, we need an even stronger program of intercollegiate athletics." For the Low Threat condition, this completed the communication. For the High Threat condition, the following sentence was added: "You, as college students, must inevitably draw the same conclusion."

The postcommunication questionnaire repeated the opinion item on de-emphasis of athletics which had appeared on the premeasure, as well as the item on importance of the issue. It also measured perceptions of the fairness of the communication, expertness of the communicator, the communicator's position, bias in his position, the extent to which he attempted to force adoption of his position, and, finally, the degree of annoyance with his conclusion.

RESULTS

Table XX classifies people according to how their opinion changed in regard to the advocated position. As may be seen, the Low Threat condition was fairly persuasive in producing positive change while the High Threat condition produced no positive trend at all. But the difference between conditions is not statistically reliable. Further inspection of the data revealed that there were several subjects who had no opinion on the issue, and who tended to see the issue as having little or no importance. For these subjects there would be little importance to freedom of opinion on the issue, and there would be little resistance to persuasion from other factors as well. These subjects do in fact show a tendency toward large positive change. When those whose initial opinion was within one point of neutral are deleted, the data appear as in Table XXI, where the expected difference between conditions is more clear, and there is even a slight boomerang tendency in the High Threat condition. The difference between conditions is significant at the 5% level by Chi-square, and a repeated measures analysis of variance shows the interaction (Before-After × Threat) to be significant at the 1% level.

There is a little increase in perceived importance of the issue in both conditions, with the High Threat condition showing somewhat more than in the Low Threat ($t = 1.38$). While no particular difference was expected, it was pointed out in Chapter I that if reactance has any effect on importance of freedom, it should be

TABLE XX

OPINION RESPONSE AS A FUNCTION OF THREAT

|  | Opinion response | | |
|---|---|---|---|
|  | Toward | No change | Away |
| Low threat | 18 | 5 | 7 |
| High threat | 11 | 8 | 11 |

TABLE XXI

Opinion Response as a Function of Threat
When Initially Neutral Subjects are Deleted

| | Opinion response | | |
| | Toward | No change | Away |
|---|---|---|---|
| Low threat | 14 | 5 | 4 |
| High threat | 7 | 8 | 11 |

to increase it. Of course, importance of the issue and importance of opinion freedom on the issue are not identical in any case.

There were no differences between conditions on the perceived fairness of the presentation, expertness of the communicator, position of the communicator, or bias in his position. But as was expected, subjects in the High Threat condition thought that the communicator tried harder to force them to adopt his position than did subjects in the Low Threat condition ($p = .02$), and they were slightly, but not reliably, more annoyed with the communicator's conclusion.

The importance of these perceptual measures of the communicator and communication is that they indicate the rather unusual technique of the communicator's telling the audience what conclusion they must draw does not seem to produce differences which would account for the obtained difference in opinion change. We cannot, of course, be sure that we have measured all of the relevant variables and for this reason some caution is appropriate in our interpretation. Nevertheless, it is apparent that the normal factors which are known to affect attitude change do not seem to account for the present results.

The major weakness of this experiment seems to be that the major finding was statistically reliable only after inspection of the data revealed that people with no initial opinion on the issue tended to be positively influenced and the data for these people were deleted. Although this adjustment makes theoretical sense, it was post hoc and the findings therefore must be replicated. For this reason, the following experiment, patterned along similar lines, was carried out by Mary L. Brehm and myself.

## Opinion Change as a Function of Communicator
## Power and Threats to Opinion Freedom

In addition to replicating the threat manipulation of the previous experiment, it was decided to examine the effect of the communicator's power relative to the audience. However, at the time this study was conducted, the way in which the communicator power variable could affect reactance was not well understood, and our predictions about its effects were quite wrong. Therefore, the analysis of the power variable effects will be post hoc, and we will not take space to spell out the incorrect predictions with which we started.

Except for the following differences, the experiment was conducted in the same way as the previously described one. The issue was the "greater use of teaching machines in education." The subjects, who were in a large lecture course in psychology at the University of Washington, were told that the Psychology Department was interested in student opinions regarding the use of teaching machines, and that experts on this issue had been asked to make statements about it in order to help the students think about the issue.

As before, the pre-questionnaire, which contained the experimental issue as well as several others, was administered several days prior to the experimental session. For the experimental session itself, students were told that the Psychology Department was interested in their reactions on issues related to education, and that when they received a copy of the forms to be handed out, they were first to read the instructions at the top, then the written statement, and finally they were to answer the questions that followed. While their names were required on the questionnaires, they were assured that their answers would be kept completely confidential and were to be used for research purposes only.

The introductory instructions for the communication reiterated that the Department had asked the opinions of experts on the issue in order to help students think about the issue. The communication was then attributed either to "a prominent educator here at the University," or to a local "high school student who received a national award for an essay on this issue." Winning the award was attributed to the high school student in order to make him appear just as expert on the issue as the professor.

The communication presented a predominance of "facts" and

arguments in favor of the use of teaching machines. Like the communication in the previous study, it presented arguments on both sides, was well-reasoned, and was non-emotional. It concluded, "I believe that teaching machines are a great asset to education and that they should be used as much as possible in educational institutions." This ended the communication in the Low Threat condition, while in the High Threat condition, the final added sentence was, "Students at the University of Washington must by all means agree." Thus, the attempt to eliminate opinion freedom was aimed specifically at the subjects.

The post-communication questionnaire included items on the issue and its importance, experience with and knowledge about teaching machines which were intended as filler items, and then questions intended to measure perceptions of the communicator and communication. These will be described with the results.

RESULTS

In confirmation of our expectations in regard to subjects with initially neutral opinions (within one point of the neutral position), 14 out of 18 showed opinion change toward the advocated position. Since they were somewhat unevenly distributed among conditions and could therefore affect the pattern of results, they are again deleted from the analysis. Table XXII shows the frequency and direction of opinion change in each condition. It will be seen that where the

TABLE XXII

OPINION RESPONSE AS A FUNCTION OF COMMUNICATOR AND THREAT

|  | Opinion response | | |
|  | Toward | No change | Away |
| --- | --- | --- | --- |
| Professor | | | |
| Low threat | 13 | 3 | 5 |
| High threat | 6 | 1 | 8 |
| High school student | | | |
| Low threat | 15 | 0 | 6 |
| High threat | 12 | 0 | 2 |

communicator was a professor, the Low Threat communication produced positive change and the High Threat produced a very slight boomerang effect. This difference is reliable at better than the 10% level by Chi-square, and better than the 1% level by analysis of variance. This outcome, it should be noted, is quite similar to that for the previous experiment.

However, the results where the communicator was a high school student are quite different. It had originally been expected that the low power communicator's attempted elimination of opinion freedom would be seen as less appropriate than that of the high power communicator, and because of this, it was expected that the reactance effects on opinion change would be greater for the high school student communicator. The results in Table XXII indicate that the High Threat communication actually produces slightly more positive change toward the advocated position than does the Low Threat communication, though, of course, this difference is nowhere near significance. While these disconfirmatory data require some explanation, let us first review the remaining information on the impressions which the subjects had of the communications and the communicators.

There were no differences as a function of either communicator or communication on perceived fairness or helpfulness of the communication, or on perceptions of the communicator's expertness or position on the issue. However, subjects were asked how appropriate it was for the communicator to make the recommendations that he did, and this revealed some differences. Generally, subjects thought the communicator's recommendations to be relatively appropriate. In one condition, however, subjects judged the recommendations as rather low in appropriateness, and this was the condition in which the high school student gave the High Threat communication. This finding clearly does not "explain" the opinion change findings in any simple way, for it is not readily apparent why opinion change in response to the communication should have been greatest in that condition in which the communicator's recommendations were seen as least appropriate. What, then, might account for these somewhat peculiar effects?

It seems plausible that when a college student receives a message from a high school student which says "you must agree" he may not take it seriously enough for it to constitute a threat to his opinion freedom. In other words, it is suggested that the communication lost its power to threaten to the extent that the conclusion was seen as relatively low in appropriateness. The conclusion was inappropriate because the threat was hollow. It is also possible, though perhaps not completely plausible, that when the high threat statement fails to arouse reactance, it is seen as a strong appeal for agreement and therefore tends to produce additional positive change. Thus, the inappropriateness of the attempted elimination of freedom by the high school student may have converted it from a threat to freedom to a strong positive appeal. Another somewhat different possibility is that when the high school student said, "must," it meant "is probably true" rather than having the imperative meaning. Of course, the data from the present study cannot test these possibilities and only further research can do so.

To sum up our research on communicator threats to freedom, in two instances it has been found that a communicator and communication which normally produce clear positive change produce a slight tendency for negative change when a freedom-threatening statement is added to the communication. This difference is not accounted for by changes in the perceived fairness of the communication, or perceived expertness or bias of the communicator. In a third instance, however, when the power of the communicator was low relative to his audience, the communication was at least as effective in producing positive opinion change when the "freedom-threatening" statement was added. In this case, the conclusion of the communicator was seen as somewhat inappropriate and may therefore have failed to constitute a real threat to freedom.

## Summary

This chapter has presented the argument that reactance can be aroused in regard to opinions and attitudes. While on the objective side it would seem that people are free to think or believe anything they want, in practice there are ubiquitous attempts to control thoughts and feelings. These attempts will tend to determine on what issues a person has freedom of thought. In general, however, we may assume that people feel freedom to select their own position in regard to attitudinal or opinion issues. The importance of the freedom to adopt or reject a given attitudinal position will depend upon how that particular position relates to important values and consequences for the individual.

When an individual feels free to adopt his own position on an issue, an attempt to force him to take a specified position or to influence him will threaten his freedom and arouse reactance. He may re-establish his freedom by avoiding opinion compliance or positive influence, and he can most clearly re-establish his freedom by moving away from the advocated position.

Data from the various experiments reported in the literature confirm the proposition that when the communicator apparently intends to influence, there is resistance to change. An experiment specifically designed for the purpose, showed that resistance to influence is not limited to influence attempts which would normally evoke implicit counterargument. Finally, two experiments were reported in which the communicator concluded by telling his audience what position they had to adopt. While in two of three instances a communicator produced less opinion change when he attempted to force the adoption of his position, in the third instance, in which the communicator's power was low relative to his audience, the attempt to force adoption did not result in less change.

# CHAPTER VII

# Resumé

In the previous chapters we have presented a theory about how behavioral freedoms come to be eliminated or threatened with elimination, and what some of the psychological consequences of such threats and eliminations may be. Without attempting to be highly systematic, we have spelled out a variety of implications of the theory, and presented relevant evidence wherever it was available. It is now appropriate to review the theory and the data collected to test it, and to attempt some appraisal and perspective. Let us begin with the review.

It is assumed that people have the subjective experience of freedom to do what they want, to do it in the way they want, and to do it when they want in regard to limited and specifiable areas of behavior. From an objective point of view, it is plausible to assume that behavioral freedom helps a person to satisfy his needs and to avoid harm and pain. On the basis of these assumptions, it is hypothesized that when a specific freedom is eliminated or threatened with elimination, the individual will be motivationally aroused to recover that freedom. The theory, then, is an attempt to specify how freedoms may be eliminated or threatened with elimination, and what the effects of the consequent motivational state, reactance, may be.

The magnitude of reactance aroused by an elimination or threat is a direct function of the following factors.

1. The absolute importance to the individual of the freedom, that is, its unique instrumental value for the satisfaction of potentially important needs.

2. The relative importance of the freedom compared to the importances of other freedoms at the time of the elimination.

3. The proportion of freedoms eliminated.

4. The elimination of freedoms by implication.

5. The magnitude of the pressure to comply when there is a threat of elimination of freedom.

When a person experiences reactance, he will tend to show the following effects:

1. Increased desire for the behavior which has been eliminated or threatened, and increased feeling of being able to have what was eliminated or threatened.

2. A tendency to engage in the threatened behavior.

3. A tendency to engage in any behavior which implies he could also engage in the threatened or eliminated behavior.

4. A tendency to encourage an "equivalent" person to engage in the threatened or eliminated behavior, or a behavior that implies he could.

As we have seen, the theory may be applied to a variety of social and non-social situations. The elimination of freedom or threat thereof may be completely fortuitous and impersonal, it may be apparently intended and personal, it can come from a source over which one has little or no power, it can come from a source over which one has great power, etc. The effects of reactance are in large part determined by the conditions under which the reactance is aroused. Only the subjective effects of increased feelings of mastery over one's fate, and increased desire for the eliminated or threatened freedom may always be expected to occur whenever reactance is aroused, and even these effects may be minimized when they clearly fly in the face of reality. Whether or not there will be attempts at direct re-establishment of behavioral freedoms will depend first, of course, on whether or not the instigating condition for reactance is characterized as an elimination or as a threat of elimination. If it is only a threat, then re-establishment may occur by the individual's engaging in the threatened free behavior. However, the individual can sometimes more easily or safely restore his freedom by engaging in a different behavior which implies he could engage in the threatened behavior. It is also possible in some situations for the individual's freedom to be re-established without his doing anything at all: that is, if a second person has been subjected to the same threat to freedom, and then if the second person engages in the threatened behavior or one which implies he could, the first individual's freedom will also be restored.

When the instigation for reactance is the elimination of a freedom, the only possibility for re-establishment of the freedom is by the indirect method of engaging in a behavior which implies that one could engage in the eliminated one. Of course, for this kind of re-establishment of freedom to occur, there must be some behavior the engaging in which would imply that one could engage in the eliminated one. Given this possibility, the individual's freedom can also be restored by another person's engaging in the behavior which implies that the eliminated behavior could be engaged in. When an individual has had a freedom eliminated by someone of relatively low power, we may expect that he will attempt to avoid recurrence of this by demonstrating his power, by increasing his surveillance over the other person, and by reducing the other person's access to things and events necessary to his freedoms.

In order to summarize the evidence, we shall list some general hypotheses from the theory and cite the findings for each.

1. *When a free behavior of an individual is eliminated, his desire for that behavior or for the object of it will increase.* Brehm, Stires, Sensenig, and Shaban (1966) showed that when the third most attractive of four records serving as choice alternatives was fortuitously and impersonally eliminated, it tended to become more attractive. Brehm, McQuown, and Shaban (Chapter II) obtained a small and unreliable tendency for increased desire to see a movie eliminated from among three movies as choice alternatives. In this case, too, the elimination was fortuitous and impersonal. That a more personal elimination of freedom has similar effects was shown by Hammock and Brehm (1966). Their experiment found that when there are only two choice alternatives and the less attractive of them is arbitrarily eliminated by an "assistant," rank preference of the eliminated item tended to increase while rank preference of the remaining gift item tended to decrease. Similar effects were obtained when the preferred alternative was eliminated.

2. *When a free behavior is threatened with elimination, the individual's desire for that behavior or its object will increase.* An experiment by Brehm and Hammock (Chapter V) found that a barrier in terms of physical distance tended to increase the attractiveness of a choice alternative but tended to have no effect on the attractiveness of an item which was not a choice alternative. However, this difference was significant at only the 12% level and must be taken as tentative.

3. *When a free behavior is threatened with elimination, the individual will tend to attempt re-establishment of freedom by engaging in the behavior which is threatened.* This hypothesis has received support in a number of ways. Burton (Chapter IV) found that in a two-alternative choice situation in which the alternatives were about equally attractive, subjects tended to select the opposite alternative to that suggested by a peer. In a similar experiment, Brehm and Sensenig (1967) showed that when subjects received a note indicating a peer was attempting to usurp their choice, they resisted this attempted influence. That a preferred alternative will be rejected if "forced" upon one was shown by Weiner (Chapter IV). Using first- and second-grade children as subjects, she found that when a subject was informed a peer said the subject *had* to take the toy he preferred out of seven, he then tended to rank that toy down in his preferences and thereby select a different one for himself. In a rather different vein, Brehm and Cole (1966) have shown that when a favor performed by one person for another threatens the latter's freedom it can reduce the tendency for the favored person to help the favorer. In yet another setting, Mary L. Brehm (Chapter VI) in one study and Mary L. Brehm and Brehm in another (Chapter VI) demonstrated that when a communicator tells his audience what conclusion they must draw, there is significant resistance to attitude change and even a tendency for boomerang attitude change. However, they also found that a low-power communicator failed to produce resistance, and effect that was not predicted, but which is nevertheless understandable in terms of the theory. All of these studies, of course, have dealt with a social threat to freedom.

Impersonal threats to freedom have also been shown to result in tendencies toward direct re-establishment of freedom. Weiner and Brehm (Chapter V) found that both verbal and monetary inducements designed to "force" shoppers to buy a specified item tended to result in resistance to the purchase of it, the effect being statistically reliable for the monetary inducement. However, the resistance effects were limited to female shoppers, the males showing no effect for the monetary inducement and increased compliance in buying the specified item for the verbal inducement. The support from this study, then, was mixed. Stronger support comes from the study by Brehm and Krasin (Chapter VI) in which college freshmen were shown to increase their resistance to influence to the point of a slight boomerang tendency as the discrepancy increased between their own opinion and that of an unidentified college student, but only when they were told they were expected to be influenced.

4. *The greater is the absolute and/or relative importance of the freedom threatened or eliminated, the greater will be the magnitude of reactance and its effects.* Two experiments have yielded support for this hypothesis while a third failed to give support. In the experiment by Brehm and Cole (1966) in which it was shown that a favor can reduce a person's tendency to be helpful toward the favorer, some subjects were given unimportant reasons for being free of obligation to the favorer, while other subjects were given important reasons. It was found that with unimportant reasons, the favor increased the likelihood of the subject's performing a return favor, while with important reasons, the favor decreased the likelihood of a return favor. In the experiment by Burton (Chapter IV), the tendency of the subject to select the opposite choice alternative to that suggested by a peer was statistically reliable only when subjects were led to believe that the choice was part of a personality test. When subjects were led to believe that the experimenter was just gathering information for future research (and that the choice was not part of a personality test), the tendency to choose the opposite alternative to that suggested was not statistically reliable.

In the first of the two experiments reported by Brehm, Stires, Sensenig, and Shaban (1966), an attempt was made to manipulate the importance of the freedom to choose any of four choice alternatives by manipulating the attractiveness of the alternatives. The manipulation, using sets of LP phonograph albums versus using sets of single 45 rpm records, failed to affect increases in the attractiveness of the eliminated record. However, this failure was probably due to the fact that the eliminated record, the third most attractive, was relatively unattractive even when it was an LP album. Of course, only further research can determine whether this interpretation is correct or the theory is incorrect in this regard. But it would seem that the present formulation in regard to the role of importance has at least some validity as seen in the previous two experiments, described above.

5. *The greater is the proportion of behavioral freedoms threatened or eliminated, the greater will be the magnitude of reactance and its effects.* Only the experiment by Brehm, McQuown, and Shaban (Chapter II) has tested this hypothesis, but it provided relatively clear support. When the second most attractive choice alternative (a movie)

was eliminated, it increased in attractiveness more when it was one of three choice alternatives than when it was one of six.

6. *The greater the number of freedoms threatened or eliminated by implication, the greater will be the magnitude of reactance and its effects.* Mixed support has been obtained for this hypothesis in the experiment by Brehm and Sensenig (1967). When subjects received a note indicating a peer was attempting to usurp their choice in a two- alternative choice situation, some were under the impression they would receive this advisory note only in regard to the first of five decisions, while others were under the impression they would receive a note for each of the five decisions. Thus, it was possible for the latter group, but not the former, to imagine that their four future decisions might also be subjected to the attempted usurpation. The results showed that the tendency to choose the opposite task to that suggested in the note was slightly greater when there was the possibility for implied usurpation in regard to future decisions. However, this effect occurred only for female subjects and even then was not statistically reliable. Thus, the evidence that implied eliminations of freedom affects the magnitude of reactance is only suggestive.

In summary, there is considerable evidence in support of the theory, and only a minor amount of disconfirmatory evidence. The evidence, as our above review shows, bears on several different propositions of the theory. Furthermore, the supporting evidence encompasses a variety of experimental settings, subjects, and operational variables. This breadth and variety of conceptual and empirical support give us added confidence that there is some validity in at least the central proposition of the theory. That is, we would conclude, at least tentatively, that people are motivationally aroused by the elimination or threat of elimination of a behavioral freedom, and tend to show increased desire for the eliminated or threatened behavior as well as attempts to engage in it.

Of course, the experiments which have been conducted to test the theory do not constitute completely unequivocal evidence. As with all research, it is possible to construct one or more alternative explanations for each and every piece of supporting data, and some of the experiments are weaker than others in this respect. While we have made every effort to rule out alternative interpretations as they have occurred to us, only critical appraisal over a period of time can determine the degree to which this effort has been successful.

There is obvious need for further testing of the basic notion that elimination of freedom is motivationally arousing, as there is need for tests of the various propositions about what controls the magnitude of reactance and what effects may occur. In particular, the propositions that reactance can be aroused by implication, and especially social implication, and the coordinate propositions that freedom can be re-established by implication and, again, social implication, need thorough empirical investigation. Indeed, many of the more interesting ramifications of the theory would seem to be those complicated ones from which we have shied in our attempts to obtain relatively unequivocal tests of the basic formulation.

## SOME CONCEPTUAL PROBLEMS

The usefulness of a theory is directly related to its conceptual clarity. The present theory can prove useful to the extent that the concepts of "free behaviors," "threat or elimination of freedom," and "re-establishment of freedom" are defined so that they allow un-equivocal determination of operations. At the same time, there is the danger in too much precision of definition without relevant data that one will inadvertently err and produce a sterile theory. But there is a middle road which is useful for theory building: conceptual variables are defined with sufficient precision to allow experimentally contrived tests of hypotheses, although the definitions may be relatively inadequate for the analysis of data gathered for other purposes. It is this road which we have tried to follow in the present work. Quite necessarily, then, there are problems of conceptualization and it may be useful to mention some of them.

First of all, it will frequently be unclear whether or not a given behavior is free to the individual. For example, if a college student volunteers to participate in an experiment and is then told by the experimenter that he is free to choose between two tasks, does he necessarily have that freedom? We have seen, of course, in several experimental tests that if the subject's choice is threatened with usurpation by a peer, he acts as if he thought he had the freedom. But suppose the experimenter usurps the subject's choice. Will the subject then experience reactance? It seems doubtful that he would because in volunteering for the project, he has put himself at the disposal of the experimenter. Within a rather large range of things which may be asked of him in connection with the experiment, he has no freedom. So if the experimenter wishes to withdraw any freedom after having given it, the experimenter may be able to do so without arousing reactance. Strictly speaking, however, the theory would lead one to believe that once the freedom was given, elimination of it would necessarily arouse reactance. Perhaps one should say of the example that reactance is aroused but only minimally since the importance of this freedom would be slight. As may be seen, we have no definitive way of handling this problem, nor may the problem be seen as highly atypical. More generally, it is not clear how much convincing a person needs through formal agreement or through experience to establish that he has a certain freedom.

A second conceptual unclarity has to do with the re-establishment of freedom. Various relatively unequivocal ways in which one might attempt to re-establish his freedom have been pointed out and illustrated with research evidence. For the sake of clarity and brevity in our discusssion, the more subtle and complicated possibilities for the re-establishment of freedom have been ignored. But it should be noted that the definition of re-establishment may eventually encompass purely cognitive change as well as overt behavior. For example, it seems quite plausible that a person may frequently be content to convince himself that he *could* engage in the threatened or eliminated behavior if he wanted to (but he simply does not care *that* much about it). This is a rather important point because the theory deals with freedom and its elimination, not behavior and its elimination, and while engaging in the relevant behavior yields excellent evidence that one has the freedom to do so, there are other ways of determining whether or not one has that freedom. Thus, the individual may be satisfied to learn that the elimination is illegal or not enforceable, or he may be satisfied by learning that a sizable group of peers agrees with him and will not tolerate a given elimination (even though none actually engages in the eliminated or threatened behavior). In short, the overt re-establishment of freedom may occur much less frequently than cognitive re-establishment even though we have formulated the theory primarily in terms of the overt. It is to be hoped that this issue can be clarified in future research.

## THE GIVING UP OF FREEDOM

There is one rather important theoretical problem which has been neglected but which deserves some discussion. It is the particular question of what happens when reactance has been aroused but the individual has been unable to re-establish the eliminated freedom. It is also the more general question of how a person changes from believing he is free to engage in some particular behavior to believing he is not free to engage in that behavior.

It is safe to assume that there is some pressure on a person to be realistic about what he can and cannot do. If it is physically impossible to engage in a given behavior, then a person must come to terms with this reality even if it were formerly possible to engage in that behavior. Similarly, if there are penalties for engaging in a certain behavior, the individual must recognize those penalties and the chances that he will have to pay them, even if the penalties have only recently been invoked. Thus, from the pressure to be realistic about one's environment, it may be expected that a person will eventually tend to give up the belief that he is free to engage in a given behavior when the re-establishment of freedom proves to be impossible.

How long it takes for one to give up a belief that he is free to engage in an eliminated behavior would presumably depend in part upon the unequivocality of the elimination. If, for example, the art museum burns to the ground, it is quite clear that the freedom to view the contents has been eliminated. Or, if the penalty for painting one's house red were made confiscation of the house, one's freedom to paint one's house red would be effectively eliminated. In both instances we might expect a fairly rapid giving up of the eliminated freedoms. But if the supply of macadamia nuts became short because of a botanical disease, the resultant threat to one's freedom to obtain these nuts would likely be so equivocal that one would not quickly give up this freedom.

At the same time, how long it takes one to give up the belief that he has a certain freedom will depend upon the magnitude of reactance aroused by the elimination since the reactance, of course, is directed against giving up the freedom. Thus, we might expect that the more important is the freedom eliminated, the fewer freedoms the person has, and the more freedoms eliminated by implication, the greater will be the magnitude of reactance and consequent resistance to giving up the freedom. Thus, given an unequivocal elimination of an important freedom, we may expect an irrational response on the part of the individual: he will show a sharp increase in his desire to engage in the eliminated behavior and he will feel that he can have or do what he wants in this regard. But in the face of the unequivocal elimination, this immediate response cannot be expected to last long. Precisely what happens to the reactance, then, is not at all clear. At least in some cases, where the individual makes an implicit decision to give up the freedom, the reactance can be conceptualized as a cognitive element dissonant (Festinger, 1957) with his decision. Thus, the greater is the reactance aroused by the elimination, the greater would be the ensuing dissonance once he decided to give up the freedom, and the more he would try to convince himself that he did not (and perhaps should not) have the freedom which was eliminated. Thus, at least in some cases, dissonance would tend to lead to rejection of the freedom. However, no general answers can be given at this time about what happens to reactance when re-establishment of freedom is impossible, nor about what factors control the giving up of behavioral freedoms.

A DEVELOPMENTAL VIEW

One's stockpile of freedoms is obviously a function of age. Neither newborn infants nor the infirm and aged have many freedoms, while somewhere in between, where a person has reached or shortly passed the peak of his physical abilities and has begun to acquire cultural power, the number of freedoms will tend to be relatively great. This is because the freedom to engage in a given behavior depends upon one's physical ability to engage in that behavior and upon the permission of others or power over others. The child gradually acquires the requisite physical abilities for various freedoms as he grows from infancy to adulthood, though, of course, there will be individual differences in endowment and development of these abilities. At the same time, permission to engage in various behaviors will be acquired, partly as a function of age and partly as a function of one's demonstrating the necessary responsibility and judgment in exercising the relevant freedom. Then, as an adult acquires occupational skills, and as he acquires power in terms of position and wealth, he will acquire additional freedoms. For example, he may become free to run for public office, to join social clubs, to travel, to send his children to college, etc.

Ultimately, the normal individual will pass his peak of physical, occupational, and social powers, though not necessarily at the same time, and his stockpile of freedoms will diminish. One of the significant points in our own culture in the diminishment of freedom is occupational retirement, which frequently is forced. At this point the individual's freedom to carry out the behaviors on which he spent the most significant part of his life are suddenly eliminated. Similar dramatic eliminations of freedom occur when an individual becomes blind, deaf, or otherwise an invalid. Eventually, then, one tends to lose many of the freedoms acquired throughout life.

One other notable aspect of the developmental process is that a person presumably learns ways of coping with reactance. For, as was noted in Chapter I, reactance and its effects are in many ways antithetical to civilization. The function of reactance is to protect the individual's freedom to do whatever he wants, and this must inevitably clash with the pressures of social life. Everyone cannot do what he wants whenever he wants if social organization and cooperation are to be maintained. While we might therefore expect considerable reactance and consequent strife in social behavior, one of the effects of civilizing the individual would be to suppress the overt and direct effects of reactance. It may be presumed that an additional effect of civilization is that the individual learns more subtle and acceptable modes of re-establishing eliminated or threatened freedoms.

In addition, the present point of view would suggest some hope for the individual's adjustment since it proposes that the individual learns what he is free to do. Thus, the mere fact that a person wants to do something should not arouse reactance and attempts to do it. Only if he has some reason to believe that he is or should be free to have something, and then does not have it, should there be reactance and its consequent effects.

A WORD OF CAUTION

The notion of freedom is rather pervasive at least in American life, and there is the consequent possibility of seeing implications of the present theory for the understanding of a wide variety of psychological phenomena. On the one hand, this pervasiveness gives the theory some generality and power, but on the other hand, it makes the theory susceptible to misuse. For as we have tried to show in the preceding pages, there is considerable overlap of the phenomena covered by the present theory and phenomena covered by theories of frustration, social influence, etc. While it is true that the present theory may prove to be a better explanation of some of these phenomena than theories which already exist, whether or not this is so can only be established by careful research. It is for this reason that in the present volume we have chosen to confine our presentation of evidence primarily to experiments explicitly designed to test the theory. Although there are many published reports of studies which might easily be explained in terms of reactance theory, other theories offer at least as adequate an explanation. In short, it is our suggestion that just as we have found it difficult to find extant tests of the theory, so it will be difficult to use reactance theory as an unequivocal explanation of a variety of phenomena.

For the unthinking researcher (no one is one, but we all know some) reactance theory is a real boon. Here at last is a theory which clearly explains why the results did not come out. Since reactance acts counter to pressure on the individual to change, obtaining no change obviously means that the pressure to change was created, but that it was cancelled out by reactance. Thus, no change on the dependent variable proves both the intended process and the reactance process as well—two birds with one stone. What could be more economical? Much as we welcome the use of reactance theory in the analysis of behavior, we hope it will be used with restraint.

Because behavioral freedom is so pervasive a part of life, and because there are many ways in which freedoms may be threatened or eliminated, if the theory is basically correct and is applied with care, it should prove to be a relatively powerful tool for the analysis of behavior. Above all, it will hopefully aid in the understanding of a wide variety of diverse and otherwise apparently unrelated phenomena.

# REFERENCES

Allyn, Jane, and Festinger, L. The effectiveness of unanticipated persuasive communications. *J. abnorm. Soc. Psychol.*, 1961, **62**, 35–40.

Brehm, J. W., and Cole, Ann. Effect of a favor which reduces freedom. *J. Pers. soc. Psychol.*, 1966, **3**, 420–426.

Brehm, J. W., and Sensenig, J. Social influence as a function of attempted and implied usurpation of choice. *J. Pers. soc. Psych.*, 1967, in press.

Brehm, J. W., Stires, L. K., Sensenig, J., and Shaban, Janet. The attractiveness of an eliminated choice alternative. *J. exp. soc. Psychol.*, 1966, in press.

Child, I. L. Childrens' preferences for goals easy or difficult to obtain. *Psychol. Monogr.*, 1946, **60** (Whole No. 280).

Child, I. L., and Adelsheim, Elizabeth. The motivational value of barriers for young children. *J. gen. Psychol.*, 1944, **65**, 97–111.

Dollard, J., Doob, L. W., Miller, N. E., Mowrer, O. H., and Sears, R. R. *Frustration and aggression.* New Haven: Yale University Press, 1939.

Festinger, L. *A theory of cognitive dissonance.* Stanford: Stanford University Press, 1957.

Festinger, L., and Maccoby, N. On resistance to persuasive communications. *J. abnorm. soc. Psychol.*, 1964, **68**, 359–366.

Freedman, J. L., and Sears, D. O. Warning, distraction, and resistance to influence. *J. Pers. soc. Psychol.*, 1965, **1**, 262–266.

French, J. R. P., Jr., and Raven, B. The bases of social power. In D. Cartwright (Ed.), *Studies in social power.* Ann Arbor: University of Michigan Press, 1959.

Hammock, T., and Brehm, J. W. The attractiveness of choice alternatives when freedom to choose is eliminated by a social agent. *J. Per.*, 1966, in press.

Heider, F. *The psychology of interpersonal relations.* New York: Wiley, 1958.

Horwitz, M. The veridicality of liking and disliking. In R. Tagiuri and L. Petrullo (Eds.), *Person perception and interpersonal behavior.* Stanford: Stanford University Press, 1958.

Hovland, C. I., Janis, I. L., and Kelley, H. H. *Communication and persuasion.* New Haven: Yale University Press, 1953.

Irwin, F. W., Armitt, F. M., and Simon, C. W. Studies in object preferences I: the effect of temporal proximity. *J. exp. Psych.*, 1943, **33**, 64–72.

Irwin, F. W., Orchinik, C. W., and Weiss, J. Studies in object preferences: the effect of temporal proximity upon adults' preferences. *Amer. J. Psychol.*, 1946, **59**, 458–462.

Janis, I. L. Motivational factors in the resolution of decisional conflicts. In M. R. Jones (Ed.), *Nebraska symposium on motivation.* Lincoln: University of Nebraska Press, 1959.

Kiesler, C. A., and Kiesler, Sara B. Role of forewarning in persuasive communications. *J. abnorm. soc. Psychol.*, 1964, **68**, 547–549.

McGuire, W. J., and Millman, Susan. Anticipatory belief lowering following forewarning of a persuasive attack. *J. Pers. soc. Psychol.*, 1965, **2**, 471–479.

McGuire, W. J., and Papageorgis, D. Effectiveness of forewarning in developing resistance to persuasion. *Publ. Opin. Quart.*, 1962, **26**, 24–34.

Mills, J. Opinion change as a function of the communicator's desire to influence and liking for the audience. *J. exp. soc. Psychol.*, 1966, **2**, 152–159.

Mills, J., and Aronson, E. Opinion change as a function of the communicator's attractiveness and desire to influence. *J. Pers. soc. Psychol.*, 1965, **1**, 173–177.

Thibaut, J. W., and Kelley, H. H. *The social psychology of groups.* New York: Wiley, 1959.

Torrance, E. P. An experimental evaluation of "no-pressure" influence. *J. appl. Psychol.,* 1959, **43**, 109–113.

Torrance, E. P., and Mason, R. Instructor effort to influence: an experimental evaluation of six approaches. *J. educ. Psychol.,* 1958, **49**, 211–218.

Walster, Elaine, and Festinger, L. The effectiveness of "overheard" persuasive communications. *J. abnorm. soc. Psychol.,* 1962, **65**, 395–402.

Wright, H. F. The influence of barriers upon the strength of motivation. Unpublished Ph. D. dissertation, Duke University, 1934.

# Author Index

# Subject Index

Choice situation
  analyzed, 18-19, 42
Commitment, 12, 15
Conceptual problems, 124-125
Counterpower, 13

Effects of reactance, 9-11
  annoyance, 69
  importance, 11, 111-112
  re-establishment of freedom
    by implication, 10-11, 41, 52, 53,
     119, 124
    direct, 9, 10, 119, 125
     by achievement, 73-74, 76-78
     by demonstration of power, 41,
      120
     by movement, 73
     by negative attitude change,
      95ff, 121
     by noncompliance, 52-54, 55ff,
      63ff, 119, 121, 122
     by surveillance of others, 41,
      120
    restraint against, 53
    subjective, 9-10, 40-41, 119, 120, 122
Elimination of freedom
  by irreversible act, 39
  by social power, 38-39
  justification of, 7-9, 17-18
  legitimacy of, 7-9

Free behaviors
  as function of development, 127-128
  defined, 3-4, 124-125
  giving up, 125-127

regarding natural events, 71-72
regarding opinions and attitudes, 92,
  95-96
regarding thoughts and feelings,
  91-92
Freedom
  benefits, 1-2, 118
  objective, 1, 118
  subjective, 1, 118
Frustration, 3, 12, 19-20, 36, 41-42,
  45, 48

Importance of freedom, 4-6, 17,
  111-112
  absolute, 4-5, 18-19, 20ff, 31, 46,
    66ff, 80, 118, 122
  in choice, 18, 42, 55ff, 63
  of opinions and attitudes, 92, 95
  relative, 5-6, 18-19, 31, 42ff, 118,
    122
Imputation of motives, 14-15, 17, 18,
  39-40, 48-49, 52, 65, 68-70, 103,
  104, 108-109, 112, 115

Opposing forces, 12

Personal weight, 13

Reactance, defined, 2, 4, 11, 118, 124
Reactance, magnitude of (*see* Threat
  to freedom), 4-7, 118-119, 124
  as function of:
    proportion of freedom eliminated,
     6-7, 29ff, 119, 122-123
    threat of elimination, 6-7, 65ff,
     119

134